Become a
VLOOKUP KnowItAll

Peter Globus

Copyright © 2017 by Peter Globus

All rights reserved. No part of this publication may be reproduced, distributed, or transmitted in any form or by any means, including photocopying, recording, or other electronic or mechanical methods, without the prior written permission of the publisher, except in the case of brief quotations embodied in critical reviews and certain other noncommercial uses permitted by copyright law. For permission requests, write to the author at *info@notadatascientist.net*

Disclaimer

Although the author has made every effort to ensure the information and examples in this book were correct at press time, the author does not assume, and hereby disclaims, any liability to any party for loss, damage, or disruption caused by errors or omissions, whether such errors or omissions result from negligence, accident, or any other cause.

Cover Illustration by Denis Ismagilov

Cover design by Peter Globus

Editing, book design by Crys Wood – papercranepublishing.com

ISBN-10: 1976332885
ISBN-13: 978-1976332883

To my wife, Lizzy

for supporting all my crazy ideas.

CONTENTS

INTRODUCTION — 1

VLOOKUP BASICS — 3

The Structure of a VLOOKUP — 5

Lookup Value — 5

Table Array — 6

Column Index — 6

Range — 6

Basic Knowledge — 7

Summary — 8

Quick Quiz — 9

Quick Quiz Answers: VLOOKUP Basics — 10

LOOKUP VALUE — 11

Literal Lookup Value — 11

Literally No Quotes — 13

Referenced Value — 14

Operational Lookup Values — 16

Concatenate VLOOKUP — 17

Store Report — 18

Resident Parking Report — 20

Summary	22
Something to consider:	22
Quick Quiz	23
Quick Quiz Answers: Lookup Value	24

TABLE ARRAY   25

Table Array from Far Away	27
Table Array from Even Farther Away	30
Table Array by Column Only	31
Being Indirect	32
Summary	32
Quick Quiz	33
Quick Quiz Answers: Table Array	34

COLUMN INDEX   36

Outlaw Calculations Report	37
Remember Your ABCs	37
Tricks for Counting Columns	38
Using a Header Value	39
Summary	40
Quick Quiz	41
Quick Quiz Answers: Column Index	42

RANGE   43

Rules for Ranges #1: No Gaps	45
Rules for Ranges #2: Ascending Order	45
Rules for Ranges #3: Descriptive Values to the Right	45
Numeric Ranges	46
Summary	47
Quick Quiz	47
Quick Quiz Answers: Range	48

MAKING MISTAKES – ERROR MESSAGES   49

#N/A Error	49
#REF! Error	52
#VALUE! Error	52
Other Common Pitfalls	52
Summary	54
Quick Quiz	54
Quick Quiz Answers: Making Mistakes – Error Messages	56

HANDLING ERRORS GRACEFULLY   57

Avoiding the #N/A Result	58
Addition with IFERROR	60
Using IFERROR Rather Than ISNA	61
A Word of Caution	61
Summary	62

Quick Quiz	62
Quick Quiz Answers: Handling Errors Gracefully	64

RELATIVE AND ABSOLUTE REFERENCES — 65

Chicken and Egg	66
Rock, Paper, Scissors	67
Introducing the Dollar Sign	70
Multiplication Table	72
Summary	75
Quick Quiz	76
Quick Quiz Answers: Relative and Absolute References	78

THE MATCH FUNCTION — 79

MATCH and VLOOKUP	80
Runners Club Report	81
Why It Works	83
Summary	83
Quick Quiz	84
Quick Quiz Answers: The MATCH Function	86

APPENDIX - OTHER TIPS AND TRICKS — 87

Searching with Wildcards	87
Cleaning Data	88
Using a Column Index Array	89

Copying and Pasting Quickly	90
Converting Numbers to Text	91
Is There an HLOOKUP?	93
VLOOKUP Usage in VBA	93

CONCLUSION 95

INTRODUCTION

How well do you do understand the VLOOKUP function? Really? Do you understand each piece of the puzzle that makes up this powerful function? Can you quickly identify the flaw when it does not work? This book walks through both of these in detail – and more! – with multiple examples.

If you had not heard of VLOOKUP until you saw this book, then welcome. If you feel comfortable writing a VLOOKUP, but do not fully understand how it works, then this book is well worth reading. The advanced topics covered here are suitable for anyone who wants to know everything they can about VLOOKUP. Reading this book qualifies you as a candidate to become a VLOOKUP KnowItAll.

Will there be examples so the reader can play along at home? Yes! Throughout the book, I will reference a free companion file available for download here »

http://bit.ly/vlookupknowitall

Within that file are examples to work on so you can better understand the concepts we will cover. I strongly recommend using it.

When someone asks, "How well do you know Excel?" and the response is "Moderate-to-expert," a VLOOKUP-related question is frequently the follow-up. In some circles, it is considered part of the more advanced group of functions used within the Excel application.

"If you learn VLOOKUP, you will come to understand the deepest secrets of the universe," said no one ever. Applications and functions in Excel are like tools you have at your disposal with which to work, and VLOOKUP is a valuable tool to possess. It cannot guarantee you money, happiness, or VIP access to swanky dives. So, what then can it offer?

At its most basic level, VLOOKUP lowers the risk of data entry errors when transcribing data from one place to another. VLOOKUP can save time when copying and transferring data between reports. It can also point to data in a file and easily update changes when, and if, they happen.

When used effectively, VLOOKUP can unlock the understanding of relationships between different sets of information. There are "Aha!" moments when working in Excel, and the VLOOKUP function is a common method for exploring these connections. While it may not provide the answer to the meaning of life, VLOOKUP can provide clarity to some burning questions.

This book will walk you, the reader, through each section of this critical Excel function. Explanation of the material leverages relatable allegories, together with examples and practice problems. The objectives are to lay the foundation of how the function works and to expand on how to approach the formula when you need it.

We will start with the basic concept of how to write a VLOOKUP function, and then we will lift up the hood to see what makes it work. After we get our hands dirty with that, we will wash up and have a quick snack, at which point we will explore some more advanced VLOOKUP techniques. We will encounter VLOOKUP methods used by professionals, and we will push the limits of what is possible with this versatile function.

The intention is to start simple, then build up to learning more complex concepts and understanding when and how to apply them.

Throughout this book, examples and exercises are there to help you learn as you go. The book is designed to meet the needs of beginners while providing deeper knowledge of the subject to intermediate users. If you ever feel like you have grasped the concept being presented at the time, feel free to go on to the next section.

So, let's begin!

VLOOKUP BASICS

An Excel worksheet in Microsoft Office 2016 consists of roughly 17 million boxes called *cells*. As an Excel user, you can use a cell to record how many pushups you did this morning or any other number, letter, or combination thereof.

You can also enter a formula (also referred to as a *function* throughout this book). That means you can add some information and then get back some information.

VLOOKUP is one of these functions. The main use of VLOOKUP is to match data with common information. For example, if one Excel file contains hundreds of zip codes but no cities, we can use VLOOKUP to match and populate the city names using another file with a list of both zip codes and cities.

The VLOOKUP Function is an extremely powerful and versatile way to use Excel. You can use it to find a matching data point from another table and then perform mathematical calculations with the results. You can also mash results together in many other ways.

So, how do we call the VLOOKUP function? As for all functions in Excel, we start with an equal sign (=) in a cell.

WAIT! You might be accustomed to using a Function Arguments box like this one.

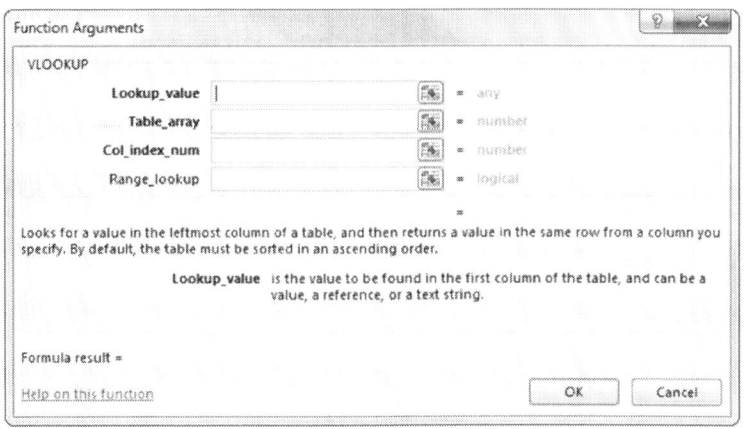

Figure 1: VLOOKUP's Function Arguments box (I recommend against using)

While I cannot stop you from using the Function Arguments box, the purpose of this book is to sharpen your Excel skills and prepare you for work in a professional setting. If you use VLOOKUP on occasion, using the arguments box is acceptable. If you use VLOOKUP and other functions frequently, your productivity will suffer by using this method.

I recommend typing the information into the cell so you can see the syntax you are using. You might ask, "What if I make a mistake?" Of course, you will! Making mistakes is extremely valuable, and the arguments box does not allow you to make egregious errors.

When you rode your bike with training wheels, bowled with bumpers, or wore a napkin like a bib, there was a point when you decided to stop. Please make that conscious decision now with regard to VLOOKUP's Function Arguments box.

Formulas and functions are ways we communicate with Excel to get the answers we are seeking. Often functions require *arguments* or *parameters*. These are pieces of information that Excel requires to understand exactly what we are looking for.

The Structure of a VLOOKUP

THE FOUR VLOOKUP ARGUMENTS

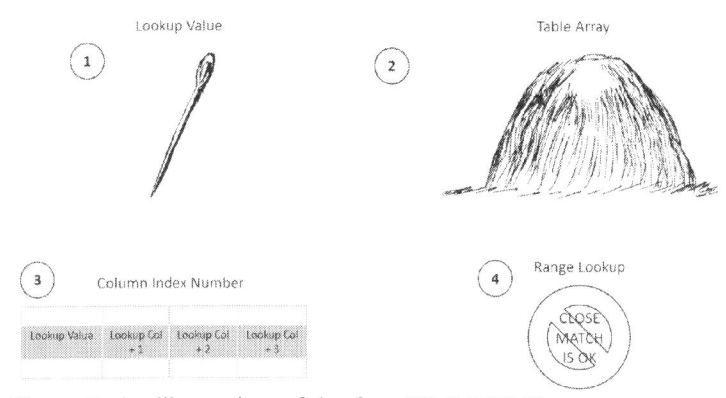

Figure 2: An illustration of the four VLOOKUP arguments

When writing a VLOOKUP function, always keep in mind:

1. The needle – *What am I seeking?*
2. The haystack – *Where am I looking for it?*
3. The column index – *What is the distance from my "needle" to the column with the answer?*
4. The range lookup – *Am I using a range of values or not?*

I created the preceding diagram to provide some additional visual context. These four parameters are the nuts and bolts of the VLOOKUP function. I will provide a brief overview describing these components, then we will dive into the details of each in the chapters that follow.

Lookup Value

The first parameter we provide is the *lookup value* – our needle. The lookup value is the identifying information for the row we are trying to match.

Picture a grade school attendance booklet with student names down the left side and dates across the top. Each day, missing students are marked absent with a capital A in that date's column and their individual rows. If we are looking at the booklet and want to see if Billy was absent last week, we would start by looking for the row with Billy's name in it. In this case,

Billy is the lookup value.

Table Array

The second parameter is the table array, illustrated earlier as a haystack. This defines the search area.

The table array consists of beginning and end points – two cell addresses separated by a colon (:), where the first address identifies the top left cell and the second address marks the cell at the bottom right. If we enter M45:P50 as the parameter for the table array, then Excel will look at the following cells in our VLOOKUP function:

```
M45 N45 O45 P45
M46 N46 O46 P46
M47 N47 O47 P47
M48 N48 O48 P48
M49 N49 O49 P49
M50 N50 O50 P50
```

Column Index

The third parameter is the column index. It is the number of columns to count, beginning from the left side of the search area. It tells Excel that once my lookup value is found in the leftmost column, move that many cells to the right – on that specific row – to find the answer.

If the lookup value describes which floor to press on an elevator, and the table array describes which building we need to be in, the column index tells us what number is on the door.

Column index is the number of columns to count from the left side of the table.

Range

The fourth parameter is the range, and it tells Excel whether we are using VLOOKUP to determine if our value is either within a specified range of values or an exact match. At this point, we will use 0 or FALSE for this argument to seek out an exact match. Later in the book, we will cover the details related to a VLOOKUP range argument with a 1 or TRUE value, although its use is limited.

With any function in the formula bar, if you point anywhere inside the parentheses, you will notice the parameters of the function displayed beneath it. To identify a parameter as optional, Excel puts brackets ([ ]) around it.

```
fx    =VLOOKUP(A2,B1:D25,2,0)
   C   VLOOKUP(lookup_value, table_array, col_index_num, [range_lookup])
```

Figure 3: Helpful text displayed beneath the formula bar

As you just learned, VLOOKUP requires a lookup value to search for, a table array to reference, the column index within that table, and a range. Notice that last parameter in the preceding illustration ([range_lookup]), which Excel is telling us is optional, but it is not. In this case, *don't believe it*. You will see why when we look more closely at the range parameter.

Basic Knowledge

When working with VLOOKUP functions, it is important to know and remember the next four points. They will help maintain your sanity and possibly assist your troubleshooting if the value returned is unexpected:

1. **VLOOKUP only searches from left to right.** There is no option to search from right to left. Excel will only find the lookup value if it exists in the leftmost column of the table array. If the lookup value is in a column to the right of the value you want to return, you will need to copy the lookup value's column to the right of your table or use other methods discussed later.

   Looking at the following illustration, this means if the Status column has the information you want to be returned and the Book column contains your lookup value, then to access the information in the Status column with VLOOKUP, you must copy it into or after column C so the Book column is first in the table array.

Copy from here   **Paste here**

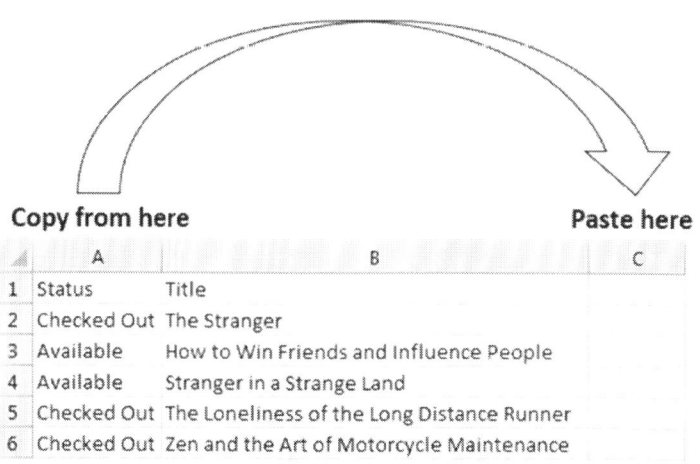

	A	B	C
1	Status	Title	
2	Checked Out	The Stranger	
3	Available	How to Win Friends and Influence People	
4	Available	Stranger in a Strange Land	
5	Checked Out	The Loneliness of the Long Distance Runner	
6	Checked Out	Zen and the Art of Motorcycle Maintenance	

Figure 4: Copying and pasting the Status column so the lookup value column (Book) will come first

2. **VLOOKUP is lazy.** It always returns the first match in the table. If there are three or four occurrences of the lookup value in the column, only the first row with matching information will be returned.

   That means if a class list has two students named Charles, using VLOOKUP to find the second student on the list will not work. Again, based on your needs, there are methods to work around this, such as searching for the students' full names by joining (or *concatenating*) the first and last names. For more on this method, see the "Concatenate VLOOKUP" section.

3. **VLOOKUP is not case sensitive.** If you look for "POND SCUM" and "pond scum" (or "Pond Scum") is on the list, VLOOKUP will return that row.

4. **VLOOKUP's fourth parameter, range lookup, can be misleading.** Most matches you look for will be exact matches, which requires you to use 0 or FALSE for this parameter. Omitting the range argument will imply that its value is TRUE and open up the possibility for problems. Does it matter whether you use 0 or FALSE? No, it is simply a matter of preference.

Summary

This chapter provided an overview of the VLOOKUP function. We covered:
- A needle-and-haystack metaphoric approach

- General information regarding the lookup value, table array, column index, and range
- Basic points to know when using VLOOKUP
- The next four chapters will dive deeper into each of the arguments in the VLOOKUP function. The first argument we will encounter is the Lookup Value.

Quick Quiz

1. How many parts are there to the VLOOKUP function?

2. What terms will this book use to refer to the parts mentioned in Question 1?
    - A. arguments or parameters
    - B. arguments or links
    - C. parameters or objects
    - D. objects or links

3. List all the parts of the VLOOKUP function.

4. True or False: Using VLOOKUP to find "ANTARCTICA" is the same as using VLOOKUP to find "Antarctica".

5. True or False: The range of the VLOOKUP function defaults to False when left blank.

Quick Quiz Answers: VLOOKUP Basics

1. How many parts are there to the VLOOKUP function?

   Four: lookup value, table array, column index, and range

2. What terms will this book use to refer to the parts mentioned in Question 1?
   - A. **arguments or parameters**
   - B. arguments or links
   - C. parameters or objects
   - D. objects or links

3. List all the parts of the VLOOKUP function.

   lookup value, table array, column index, and range

4. True or False: Using VLOOKUP to find "ANTARCTICA" is the same as using VLOOKUP to find "Antarctica".

   True: VLOOKUP is not case sensitive

5. True or False: The range of the VLOOKUP function defaults to False when left blank.

   False: The range defaults to True. Always add a zero or FALSE.

LOOKUP VALUE

Have you ever gone to get food from a concession stand at a game or a concert? When you came back and gazed at the sea of people, how did you know where you were sitting? You may have looked at your ticket to find your section and row number. You may have seen the goofy hat your friend insisted on wearing. You may have noticed the people seated nearby who introduced themselves before you ran to get refreshments. The lookup value operates in a similar way.

The lookup value, shown earlier as the needle in Figure 2, is the basis for our search. This grounding detail enables Excel to identify the row where we are looking for data.

Literal Lookup Value

The simplest form of lookup value is the literal lookup value. This means you enter the exact value for which you are looking.

For example: If I am looking for shoes, I would type in shoes. If I am looking for fish, I would type in fish. If I am looking for fish shoes, then I would likely not find any because fish have no feet … but I digress.

When entering a literal value as a lookup value, it is just that – literally entering what we are seeking. Now, I will literally show you what I mean in the following example.

If you are using the book's companion file, go to the worksheet named Palindromes, which has a list of people at the beginning of a row and those sitting next to them. If you have not downloaded the file yet and want to now, here is the download link one more time:

http://bit.ly/vlookupknowitall

The following illustration represents the concert comparison I made at the beginning of the chapter. People are sitting in seats represented by cells and in rows represented by, well, rows. Column A contains the name of the person sitting in the aisle seat at the beginning of the row. Coincidentally, each of their names is a palindrome, the point of which escapes me.

	A	B
1	Beginning of Row	Next Seat
2	Otto	Jordan
3	Sylys	George
4	Hannah	Peter
5	Anna	Victor
6	Ava	Jen
7	Elle	Larry
8	Bob	Yvette
9	Eve	Josephine
10	JJ	Eleanor

Figure 5: The Palindromes worksheet

Consider typing this formula into cell E5:

=VLOOKUP("Hannah",A1:B10,2,0)

The characters Hannah are the literal reference we are looking up. If I was returning from the restroom and the usher asked where I was sitting, and I yelled, "Hey, Hannah!" then I would be looking for my seat using a similar method. It is effective, although not the way a professional usher would expect you to find your seat.

When referring to a literal reference, we are spelling out the lookup value within the VLOOKUP formula by putting a term in quotation marks and placing it into the formula, like "Hannah".

If we type this formula in cell E3:

=VLOOKUP("Eve",A1:B10,2,0)

The result will be Josephine. The lookup value here is Eve and, once again, it is a literal reference. Therefore, literal references are taking the actual

reference.
What lookup value would you use to see George as a result? Try one or two more and then we will look at another example of a literal lookup value.

An important note is that your lookup value always comes from the first column of the table array. If we wanted to use Yvette from column B as my lookup value, we would need to change the table array accordingly, as shown earlier in Figure 4. With the Palindromes worksheet's current arrangement, there is no VLOOKUP method we can use to return Bob by using Yvette.

Literally No Quotes

You may believe the rule is to place all literal references in quotation marks, but you would believe something untrue, and you will stand corrected. There are times we use quotation marks, and there are times we do not.
For character (a single letter or a number to be treated as text) or any string (a geek word for a cluster of characters), we surround our lookup value with quotation marks (" "). When searching using a numeric value, we do not use quotation marks.

Now, go to the worksheet named Photographic Memory in the companion file.

	A	B
1	Seat	Occupant
2	103	Jordan
3	203	George
4	303	Peter
5	403	Victor
6	503	Jen
7	603	Larry
8	703	Yvette
9	803	Josephine
10	903	Eleanor

Figure 6: The Photographic Memory worksheet

If I possessed a photographic memory, was at the stadium with my hands full of goodies from the refreshment stand, and recalled my seat number from memory, I would tell the usher, "I am in seat 303." The VLOOKUP for that would look like this:

=VLOOKUP(303,A1:B10,2,0)

This is because numeric values do not require quotation marks. If we use quotations marks and type:

=VLOOKUP("303",A1:B10,2,0)

Excel will return an error indicating the value cannot be found. When we use quotation marks, Excel thinks we are speaking in text, not numbers. Make sure whichever is in the lookup value – a numeric value or a number treated as text – matches the cell contents you are referencing.

At this point, we know we can use VLOOKUP with a literal lookup value, and this value can be text or numeric. We also know several names that are palindromes, and some of my friends with these names spell them backward.

Referenced Value

If you said you were unimpressed with literal references, I would agree. By itself, a literal reference has little practical use, and I do not see how my life will be stress-free or enlightened when utilizing literal references in VLOOKUP. But, what if I use lookup value to demonstrate something more profound? What if I introduce a method to avoid typing every lookup value into a cell? I will show you what I just described now. Bring in the referenced value.

A referenced value uses a reference to a cell – instead of a literal value – as the lookup value. Essentially, we're pointing to a cell and declaring, "I want to find a cell matching the contents of this cell," instead of typing it in. We will return to the Palindromes worksheet to illustrate this.

Follow these instructions to set up the worksheet.
1. Select cell A4 and copy its contents.
2. Select cell D5 and paste into that cell.

    Hannah should now appear in cell D5.

3. Now type the following into cell E5:

$$=VLOOKUP(D5,A1:B10,2,0)$$

	A	B	C	D	E
1	Beginning of Row	Next Seat			
2	Otto	Jordan			
3	Sylys	George			
4	Hannah	Peter			
5	Anna	Victor		Hannah	Peter
6	Ava	Jen			
7	Elle	Larry			
8	Bob	Yvette			
9	Eve	Josephine			
10	JJ	Eleanor			

Figure 7: The Palindromes worksheet after adding the VLOOKUP formula

By using D5 as the first argument of the VLOOKUP, you told Excel to use the contents of cell D5 as the lookup value rather than the literal value Hannah. You pointed to Hannah by using D5 rather than typing out the name. This is a more standard method for using VLOOKUP.

What is the difference?

Type Elle into cell D5. As we see in the following illustration, Peter is replaced by Larry in cell E5. This happens because cell D5 now contains Elle, not Hannah. The formula is neutral to whatever value is in the referenced cell, and the contents of D5 dictate the value in E5. If we changed D5 to Anna, then the value in E5 would change to Victor.

	A	B	C	D	E
1	Beginning of Row	Next Seat			
2	Otto	Jordan			
3	Sylys	George			
4	Hannah	Peter			
5	Anna	Victor		Elle	Larry
6	Ava	Jen			
7	Elle	Larry			
8	Bob	Yvette			
9	Eve	Josephine			
10	JJ	Eleanor			

Figure 8: VLOOKUP referencing cell D5 in Palindromes worksheet

Now, type the name Otto into cell D9 to demonstrate another point. Referenced lookup values provide a lot of flexibility in terms of pulling data together from multiple sources. Note that we do not need to keep our referenced value adjacent to our VLOOKUP formula. We can call our reference from anywhere to obtain a value.

If we type the following in cell Z35, we will still get a result:

=VLOOKUP(D9,A1:B10,2,0)

	Z	AA	AB
35	=VLOOKUP(D9,A1:B10,2,0)		

Figure 9: A reference can be called from anywhere in the worksheet

Can you guess the value?

We are referencing cell D9, so we will get the name next to Otto. The name next to Otto in cell A2 is Jordan, and Jordan is the value returned.

We can place D9 – the needle – anywhere. In this case, the needle is a cell pointing to Otto. Cells A1 through B10 are the table array – or haystack – and the column index (2) instructs Excel to look two columns to the right starting from, and including, column A. This is why the result is Jordan.

Try this in any empty cells within the Palindromes worksheet to see if you can replicate this. For example, how can you get the name Jordan as a result in cell BE389?

Now replace the name Otto with =A2. Look back at cell Z35, and you'll see that Jordan shows as the value. We can see from here that a reference to a reference is also valid as a lookup value.

Operational Lookup Values

See the Colors worksheet named for this section.

D3				fx	=VLOOKUP(A2/B6,F2:G9,2,0)	
	A	B	C	D	E	F	G
1	1st Numb	2nd Number					
2	10	1				1 blue
3	12	2		red		2 red
4	15	3		orange		3 orange
5	24	4				4 purple
6	32	5				5 green
7	36	6				6 yellow
8	40	7				7 white
9	42	8				8 black

Figure 10: In the Colors worksheet, running operations in the lookup value argument

We can use a mathematical equation as a lookup value, too. In the preceding illustration, cell A2 (10) is divided by cell B6 (5) to get 2. The table array at right has a number 2 in cell F3, adjacent to the word red in G3. Therefore the VLOOKUP in D3 displays red because:

$$=VLOOKUP(A2/B6,F2:G9,2,0)$$

is the same as:

$$=VLOOKUP(2,F2:G9,2,0)$$

What was just demonstrated here is that we can extend the lookup value to run a separate task prior to Excel evaluating the argument. In this case, we divided 10 by 5, and then Excel evaluated the 2 for the lookup value. If we typed A3/B3 (12 divided 2) into the preceding formula as the lookup value, the result would be yellow. What formula could we use to get the word orange to appear?

Running an operation is an unusual method for obtaining a lookup value. What I want to highlight is that you can push the limits of the VLOOKUP function to accomplish needed tasks in Excel. Sometimes a lookup value appears out of reach and too hard on which to rely. In these moments, remember there are many ways to get VLOOKUP to be more helpful.
You can run mathematical operations prior to passing your lookup value, and you can also run string operations, as we will see in the next section.

Concatenate VLOOKUP

For this section, refer to the Palindromes Revisited worksheet.
What if we took the names from column A of our Palindrome worksheet and split them into two cells, as shown in columns F and G of the following illustration? Could we somehow use the split values in a VLOOKUP function?

	A	B	C	D	E	F	G
1	Beginning of Row	Next Seat					
2	Otto	Jordan				Ot	to
3	Sylys	George				Syl	ys
4	Hannah	Peter				Han	nah
5	Anna	Victor				An	na
6	Ava	Jen				Av	a
7	Elle	Larry				El	le
8	Bob	Yvette				Bo	b
9	Eve	Josephine				Ev	e
10	JJ	Eleanor				J	J

Figure 11: The Palindromes Revisited worksheet with names split into columns F and G

When we want to combine two strings (remember, a string is a cluster of alphanumeric characters), we can use the ampersand symbol (&). Earlier, we executed mathematical operations with cell contents prior to passing them to the lookup value as arguments. Now we will join cell contents prior to passing the result to lookup value. Here is how to do this…

In cell D2, type:

=VLOOKUP(F2&G2,A1:B10,2,0)

This takes Ot in cell F2 and to in cell G2 and smushes (a highly technical term meaning to squeeze tightly) them together into the lookup value argument. We will get Jordan as a result.

What if we reversed the lookup argument and used G10&F10? Would that give Eleanor as a result? Why?

We can also use a referenced value combined with a literal value, like this:

=VLOOKUP(F5&"na",A1:B10,2,0)

In this formula, we referenced An in cell F5 and added the string "na" to complete Anna's name. The result of this VLOOKUP will be Victor. So, we can join (or concatenate) referenced values with literal values to pass the argument we want to the lookup value.

If you grasp everything we have done so far, you are doing great, and you should now be ready for some more complex examples. Ready?

Store Report

Please refer to the Store Report worksheet.

For this example, we will assume the role of the district store manager of a national retail chain. We requested a report on a particular product of interest. Now we have the results, and the report includes additional stores for which we are not responsible. Furthermore, the stores are listed with the word Store followed by a space before each store number, which does not match how we keep our information. In the following illustration, you can see our short list compared to the full report.

Figure 12: A short list of stores in our district and a portion of the full report we received

In order to make these two sets of data match, we need to add Store followed by a space before each store number. Instead of manually changing the contents of each of the cells on our short list, we can add it to the VLOOKUP.

In cell K2, we will type:

=VLOOKUP("Store "&J2,A1:C21,2,0)

Note the space added after the word Store to complete the string. The resulting value is 258, the units sold in Store 1323. What this example helps demonstrate is that, in addition to the narrow alphanumeric values we saw previously, Excel will accept spaces in string arguments, as well.

When it comes to spaces and special characters, be mindful that some spaces are not spaces; a space may look like a space, but it may actually be a non-printable character. The same goes for symbols and marks reserved for Excel's use, such as quotation marks. Anytime you are about to experiment with characters of this nature, do your research to ensure you are getting the results you expect.

While writing this function, I noticed that, conveniently, the word Store is spelled out in the header row (cell J1). This gives an option to reference the cell with the word Store instead of using the literal value "Store". We can update our formula in K2 with the following:

=VLOOKUP(J1&" "&J2,A1:C21,2,0)

This uses the header value Store by referencing it instead of requiring the literal reference Store. Note that the lookup value is a concatenation of the referenced cells with a space between them as a string value.
Shortcuts like these are sometimes available in tables, and they can save valuable time.

Resident Parking Report

Frequently, organizations store fragments of their data in different areas and with inconsistent methods. Sometimes it is due to silos within the company, sometimes it is deliberate for security reasons, and sometimes the intended use of the data is categorically different.

The result is that when one department needs to access another department's data, the information must first be "massaged" prior to use.

Here is an example of such a case.

Please go to the worksheet named Residents for this section.

Consider the following scenario:

At the Main Street Apartments, there are over 70 residents, but only 27 parking spaces are available in the garage. Residents have requested that the leasing staff limit the number of emails they send because each resident received an average of five emails a day during the prior month. Additionally, the premium parking spaces always cause controversy whenever mentioned to a resident who doesn't have a spot.

The staff received word this morning that the parking garage is scheduled for line repainting this Tuesday. In an effort to minimize the number of emails, and also prevent additional gripes from spot-less residents, the staff now needs to notify this select group via email.

The Parking List has the first and last names of each occupant, but no email

Become a VLOOKUP KnowItAll

address. In a separate list, the leasing office has the residents' names formatted as Last Name, First Name – note the comma and space between the last and first names – with their respective email addresses.

We can use VLOOKUP to match the email addresses, but we will need to do some string manipulation first.

	A	B	C	D	E	F	G	H
1		PARKING LIST					APARTMENT RESIDENT LIST	
2		First	Last			Name	APT UNIT	Email
3		Emma	Cruz			Smith, Gabriel	1011	g.smith1011@notarealemail.com
4		Madison	Johnson			Jackson, Sofia	1020	s.jackson1020@notarealemail.com
5		Liam	Collins			Cruz, Emma	1022	e.cruz1022@notarealemail.com
6		Martin	McGee			Johnson, Madison	1028	m.johnson1028@notarealemail.com
7		Zoe	Alberts			Harper, Olivia	1057	o.harper1057@notarealemail.com
8		Brooke	Lee			Collins, Liam	1061	l.collins1061@notarealemail.com
9		David	Moore			McGee, Martin	1065	m.mcgee1065@notarealemail.com
10		Amy	Young			Malone, Abigail	1067	a.malone1067@notarealemail.com
11		Ava	Anderson			Evans, Charlotte	1070	c.evans1070@notarealemail.com
12		Jennifer	Martin			Wallace, Michael	1073	m.wallace1073@notarealemail.com
13		Chloe	Miller			Winters, Sylvester	1080	s.winters1080@notarealemail.com
14		Alison	Williams			Green, Jeremiah	1087	j.green1087@notarealemail.com
15		Peter	Murphy			Bowie, Savannah	1106	s.bowie1106@notarealemail.com
16		Justin	Peterson			Alberts, Zoe	1108	z.alberts1108@notarealemail.com
17		Carlos	Campbell			Jones, Ursula	1114	u.jones1114@notarealemail.com
18		Logan	Butler			Lee, Brooke	1120	b.lee1120@notarealemail.com
19		Timothy	Harris			Wu, Leonard	1121	l.wu1121@notarealemail.com
20		Jared	Brooks			Preston, Joseph	1122	j.preston1122@notarealemail.com
21		Oscar	Ross			Rodriguez, Cynthia	1146	c.rodriguez1146@notarealemail.com
22		Simon	Frye			Hassan, Kyle	1153	k.hassan1153@notarealemail.com
23		Patricia	Norman			Flynn, James	1157	j.flynn1157@notarealemail.com
24		Quincy	Andrews			Nguyen, Alex	1170	a.nguyen1170@notarealemail.com
25		Archie	Primm			Muller, Chris	1171	c.muller1171@notarealemail.com
26		Andrew	Bloom			Moore, David	1174	d.moore1174@notarealemail.com
27		Richard	Forman			Young, Amy	1185	a.young1185@notarealemail.com
28		Sarah	Owens			Clark, Courtnee	1215	c.clark1215@notarealemail.com

Figure 13: A portion of the Residents worksheet and its two lists

The Parking List is in columns B through C. The list of residents with their email addresses occupies columns F through H.

We need to format the resident names in our parking list as Last Name, First Name for our lookup value. To do, this we will start with cell D3.
In cell D3, type the following:

=VLOOKUP(C3&", "&B3,F3:H74,3,0)

The first argument includes cell C3 (the last name of the resident), then a comma and a space, followed by B3 (the first name of the resident). By combining these three elements, we are able to match the contents of column B.

When choosing how to approach any lookup value, it is helpful to consider the pattern of the information at which we are looking. With this example, it was clear that the format was Last Name, First Name. In the previous example, it was based on Store followed by a space and a store number.

Any situation where you're faced with the task of pulling data together like this requires you to first evaluate how the lookup column is structured, determine if the lookup value is similar, and, if needed, change it accordingly.

Summary

This completes our section on the lookup value. We covered:
- Using a literal string – a word or words surrounded by quotation marks – to retrieve values
- Numeric values as lookup value arguments
- Referenced values, where we call a cell containing the lookup value
- Performing mathematical operations on numbers prior to using them as lookup value arguments
- Performing string manipulation on combinations of literal strings and references prior to using them as lookup value arguments

The next chapter will cover Table Arrays, the second argument in the VLOOKUP function.

Something to consider:

Can you remember a recent professional or personal situation where you would have benefited from knowing more about lookup value and some of the techniques used in this chapter? If you have, then I recommend going back and trying it. Make this information stick by applying it to real-life examples.

Quick Quiz

1. If the lookup value exists in the table array, what value will be returned using this formula?

    =VLOOKUP("Tracy",A3:F22,1,0)

2. If the name "Tracy" is a value in cell Z22, how would you write the formula from Question 1 when using Z22 as a reference value?

3. If 23 represents an integer value in a cell, what makes this formula incorrect?

    =VLOOKUP("23",Q7:Z17,4,0)

4. What does concatenate mean, and why is it important to lookup values?

For questions 5 and 6, use the following table:

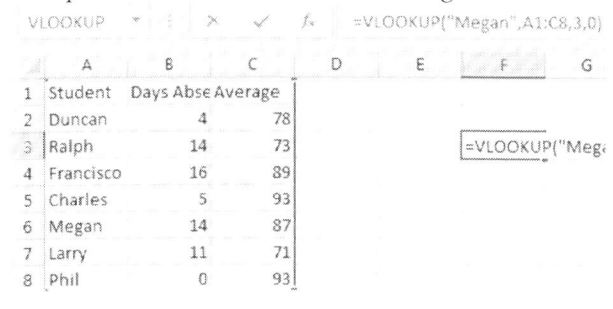

	A	B	C
1	Student	Days Abse	Average
2	Duncan	4	78
3	Ralph	14	73
4	Francisco	16	89
5	Charles	5	93
6	Megan	14	87
7	Larry	11	71
8	Phil	0	93

Formula in F3: =VLOOKUP("Megan",A1:C8,3,0)

5. Given the preceding information, what value will appear in cell F3?

6. What would the result be if you typed the following formula into cell F3?

    =VLOOKUP("Student",A1:C8,3,0)

Peter Globus

Quick Quiz Answers: Lookup Value

1. If the lookup value exists in the table array, what value will be returned using this formula?
=VLOOKUP("Tracy",A3:F22,1,0)
Tracy. 1 will always return the lookup value.

2. If the name "Tracy" is a value in cell Z22, how would you write the formula from Question 1 when using Z22 as a reference value?
=VLOOKUP(Z22,A3:F22,1,0)

3. If 23 represents an integer value in a cell, what makes this formula incorrect?
=VLOOKUP("23",Q7:Z17,4,0)
Numeric values should not be in quotation marks

4. What does concatenate mean, and why is it important to lookup values?
Concatenate means to join two or more values to use as a lookup value

For questions 5 and 6, use the following table:

	A	B	C
1	Student	Days Abse	Average
2	Duncan	4	78
3	Ralph	14	73
4	Francisco	16	89
5	Charles	5	93
6	Megan	14	87
7	Larry	11	71
8	Phil	0	93

5. Given the preceding information, what value will appear in cell F3? **87**

6. What would the result be if you typed the following formula into cell F3?
=VLOOKUP("Student",A1:C8,3,0)
Average

TABLE ARRAY

The second argument of the VLOOKUP function is the table array. We separate each argument of the formula with a comma, and the table array position follows the first comma. In the following example, it is the bold portion of the formula:

=VLOOKUP(A2&,**F2:I8**,3,0)

Figure 14: An example of a table array in cells F2 through I8

If you have ever played Battleship, you know the board consists of numbered and lettered spaces from A1 through J10. In VLOOKUP, the Battleship board could be written as A1:J10, covering 100 spaces (or cells).
In a train station, when looking at destinations, there are often track numbers, departure times, and other details as well. The entire grid is an array table that you can reference while waiting for a train.

When you think of a table, you may think of sitting at a physical table or looking at an information table, such as the periodic table of elements. The table in our definition is a specific rectangular set of cells delimited by a starting point at the top left of the table and ending at the bottom right of the table. When we provide these two cell locations to Excel, Excel figures out the cells that fall between. Tables in Excel are always rectangular (sorry King Arthur!).

The term array can describe an arrangement of flowers or a set of objects placed in a specific order. An array is also a computer-geek-speak term, and it generally means the same as our Excel definition, just defined as a set in a computer application or programming language.

This is an arranged set of numbers that is considered an array: {2, 4, 6, 8, 10}. The same could be said for the set in the following illustration (the set consists of everything inside the oval).

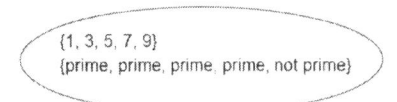

{1, 3, 5, 7, 9}
{prime, prime, prime, prime, not prime}

Figure 15: An example of a two-dimensional array – two rows and five columns

This set could be considered a two-dimensional array. The two dimensions refer to the length and height. This array has a length of 5 and a height of 2. The numeric portion of the set is aligned with the textual prime, not prime portion. A table is just a formal setup of a two-dimensional array with multiple lines.

If that seems too esoteric, just remember these two things: a table array is a haystack we are searching through to find the lookup value, and the lookup value is always in the first column of the table array.

Refer to the Planets worksheet for the following section:

Consider the following table populated with planet names and their corresponding number of moons. If we typed a VLOOKUP to include each row and column of this table, the table array would be A1:B9.

	A	B
1	Planet	Moons
2	Mercury	0
3	Venus	0
4	Earth	1
5	Mars	2
6	Jupiter	67
7	Saturn	62
8	Uranus	27
9	Neptune	14

Figure 16: The Planets worksheet

If we type Earth in cell E2, and then typed the following into cell F2:

$$=VLOOKUP(E2,A1:B9,2,0)$$

The value 1 will appear in cell F2. This is a simple example showing the use of a VLOOKUP with a table array. The table array haystack is A1:B9, and we are looking for our needle Earth, which is referenced as E2.

If we change the formula in cell F2 to the following:

=VLOOKUP(E2,A1:B3,2,0)

The cell would display #N/A for a "no value is available" error because that table array includes only the first three rows of the table (including the header row), omitting the fourth row with Earth in cell A4.

We will get another error if we change the formula in F2 to:

=VLOOKUP(E2,A1:A9,2,0)

This time, #REF! for "reference out of range" because the table array is too narrow – it only includes column A.

What if we type this into cell F2?

=VLOOKUP(E2,B1:C9,2,0)

Will it result in an error? It will, because the table array does not include column A, the column where Earth is listed.

Table Array from Far Away

We can also reference table arrays from one Excel worksheet in another Excel worksheet.

The worksheet named Planets contains a table with a list of planets. If we are working in another worksheet called Other Sheet (you will find a worksheet named Other Sheet in the book's companion file), we can write a VLOOKUP formula there that references the table in the Planets worksheet by using the table array argument: Planets!A1:B9.

	A	B	C
1	Planet	Moons	
2	Mercury	0	
3	Venus	0	
4	Earth	1	
5	Mars	2	
6	Jupiter	67	
7	Saturn	62	
8	Uranus	27	
9	Neptune	14	
10			

... | Planets | Other Sheet |

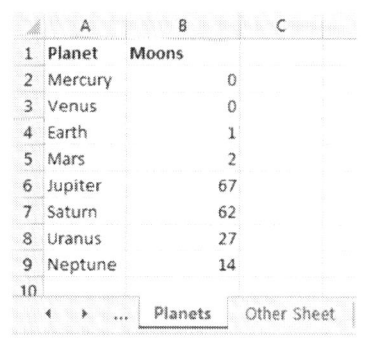

Figure 17: The Planets worksheet referenced in the next illustration

The standard method for referencing another worksheet is to use the worksheet's name followed by an exclamation mark (!). To be clear, I was not deliberately emphasizing that last sentence.

If the worksheet Other Sheet, where we are writing the VLOOKUP formula, contained a real planet's name (and not a dwarf planet like Pluto) in cell A2, and we typed the following formula into cell B2...

=VLOOKUP(A2,Planets!A1:B9,2,0)

	A	B	C	D	E
1					
2	Jupiter	=VLOOKUP(A2,Planets!A1:B9,2,0)			
3					

... | Planets | Other Sheet | Outlaws |

Figure 18: An example of referencing a table array that is located in a different worksheet

...the value will be the number of moons for Jupiter, the planet named in cell A2, which is 67.

The complexity introduced here is that our VLOOKUP function is in one worksheet, while the table array is in another. This is a powerful use of the VLOOKUP function, as you will see later.

Note that if the worksheet with the referenced table array has spaces in its name, Excel requires us to put single quotation marks (') around it. The Planet worksheet does not require these single quotation marks, but if we renamed the Planets worksheet Planet Moons, the syntax for referencing it would look like this:

=VLOOKUP(A2,'Planet Moons'!A1:B9,2,0)

Those single quotation marks are only around the worksheet name. The exclamation point is outside of the quotation marks.

We can make this easier by having Excel write the table array argument for us when we do the following:

1. In the Other Sheet worksheet, type the following into cell B3:

=VLOOKUP(

2. Point to cell A2 and select it. Notice how your action added the cell reference to the formula, which now reads:

=VLOOKUP(A2

3. Now type a comma ,
4. Then point to the Planets worksheet tab and click it. That action added the worksheet's name to the formula, which now reads:

=VLOOKUP(A2,Planets!

5. On the Planets worksheet, drag to select cells A2 through B9. The formula will now read:

=VLOOKUP(A2,Planets!A2:B9

6. Now type another comma , followed by 2,0) and press ENTER.

Do you see how Excel assisted in writing this formula? It entered the correct syntax for the worksheet name, as well as the table array, which is a great method for typing the formula without using the Formula Arguments box and without having to memorize the worksheet's name or the exact cell addresses of the table array.

Now, return to the Other Sheet worksheet and type the value Store 1644 in cell A, then use the earlier steps to see if you can have Excel write a VLOOKUP formula in cell B4 that will retrieve the value 535 from the Store Report worksheet On Hand column.

Notice that when you click the Store Report tab, the worksheet name appears in the formula surrounded by single quotation marks.

Your completed formula should look like this:

=VLOOKUP(A4,'Store Report'!A1:C21,3,0)

Table Array from Even Farther Away

Can we use a VLOOKUP from one workbook to another? I asked the question and, considering the title of this section, if you go with Yes, then you are correct.

Referencing a different workbook is similar to referencing a different worksheet. To demonstrate this, we will first create a new Excel workbook, which will be named Book1 automatically.

On a PC, the shortcut to create a new file is CTRL+N, or you can select the File menu, click New, and then click Blank Workbook.

With your new workbook open, you can enter the following in the Sheet1 worksheet:

1. In cell B2, type:

    =VLOOKUP("Mars",

2. Navigate to the book's companion Excel file and click the Planets worksheet tab.

Notice that the formula now includes the file path with the workbook's name in brackets [ ] followed by the worksheet name.

3. Now drag to select cells A1 through B9.

4. Type another comma , followed by 2,0) and press ENTER.

Figure 19: An example of referencing a table array that is located in a different file

Note that the new workbook is referencing our companion file for this information. If we save and close the companion file, our reference includes the path to the workbook. Save and close the companion file and see for yourself. Then re-open the companion file and check cell B2 on Sheet1 of Book1 again. You will see the path has disappeared again.

Table Array by Column Only

Sometimes I build a VLOOKUP with the expectation that the number of rows in the table array may increase, and sometimes (often) I am too lazy to count the rows of the table array. In either case, this is not a problem. I can abbreviate the table array argument to include an entire column.

Go to the Planets worksheet once more, and type the following into cell G2 of the Planets table:

=VLOOKUP(E2,A:B,2,0)

Note that A:B is the beginning and end of the table array, as opposed to the cell addresses A1:B9. This will set the table array as the entire length of columns A and B, from row 1 to the last row in the worksheet. Select cell G2 and you'll see all the rows in columns A and B are highlighted, as shown in the following illustration.

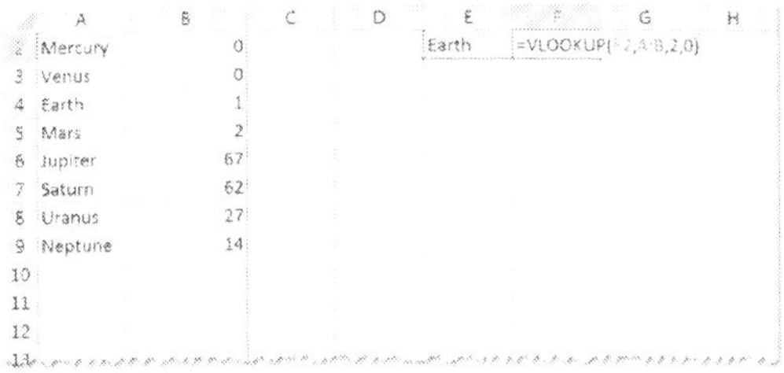

Figure 20: An example of referencing entire columns as a table array

Cell F2 should still have the formula:

=VLOOKUP(E2,A1:B9,2,0)

Now select cell F2. You'll see that the cells are highlighted only through row 9. Note the difference?

There is one thing you need to keep in mind with using full columns in table arrays: If it happened that you typed Pluto on line 736 while half-asleep, and then forgot about it, the formula's result might be unexpected. Change the value in cell E2 to Pluto and see what happens.

Keep in mind that you need to be certain the remaining rows are clear when referencing an entire column.

Being Indirect

Similar to lookup value, when populating a value inside a table array argument, we can provide a literal value or use a function called INDIRECT, which acts as a reference value.

Using our Planets worksheet again, type A1:B9 into cell E5, and then type the following formula into cell E7:

=VLOOKUP("Saturn",INDIRECT(E5),2,0)

The resulting value is 62.

By contrast, if we enter the cell address directly, like this:

=VLOOKUP("Saturn",E5,2,0)

The result will be #N/A, the "no value is available" error.

This occurs because the INDIRECT function processes the cell contents as a reference and recognizes the A1:B9 range, which it then passes to the VLOOKUP table array argument. But the VLOOKUP function cannot, by itself, process the contents of cell E5. It expects a table array, but it receives a cell address. It does not recognize E5 as a cell reference.

An important note is that the INDIRECT function does not operate on references to table arrays within closed files and will return a #N/A error in that situation. Even if you have the correct path in the function, if the referenced table array is in a closed file, VLOOKUP will return an error.

Summary

This completes our section on the table array. We covered:
- The definition of a table array
- How selecting the wrong table array returns an error
- How to select a table array located in a different Excel worksheet
- How to select a table array located in a different Excel file
- The "lazy way" to select entire columns as a table array
- Using the INDIRECT function with a table array

The next chapter will cover Column Index, the third argument in the VLOOKUP function.

Quick Quiz

1. How many columns wide is table array C3:G8?

Consider this table of coffee table specifications for questions 2 through 4:

	C	D	E	F	G
1	Name	Height	Width	Length	Material
2	The Mod	45 in	36 in	36 in	Metal/Glass
3	Rustic Root	38 in	40 in	52 in	Wood/Iron
4	Levels	48 in	48 in	62 in	Metal
5	The Chester	42 in	40 in	58 in	Wood

2. Fill in the blank to complete the following formula so it returns the value Wood:

$$=VLOOKUP(C6,C2:\_\_,5,0)$$

3. If the Height column contains our lookup value and Length is the column we plan to use for a return value, what should be our table array?

4. If cell I6 contained the value C2:G6 and we wanted to use I6 as a reference, what will our VLOOKUP statement look like if the lookup value is Rustic Root and the column index is 5?

5. How many columns are in the table array F4:Q34?

6. Why would this formula return an error?

$$=VLOOKUP(C2,D1:M6,20,0)$$

7. When and why should we use single quotation marks in a VLOOKUP formula?

8. Based on the table array syntax, is the following a valid VLOOKUP statement? Why or why not?

$$=VLOOKUP(2,D:Q,3,0)$$

Quick Quiz Answers: Table Array

1. How many columns wide is table array C3:G8? **5 columns wide**

Consider this table of coffee table specifications for questions 2 through 4:

	C	D	E	F	G
1	Name	Height	Width	Length	Material
2	The Mod	45 in	36 in	36 in	Metal/Glass
3	Rustic Root	38 in	40 in	52 in	Wood/Iron
4	Levels	48 in	48 in	62 in	Metal
5	The Chester	42 in	40 in	58 in	Wood

2. Fill in the blank to complete the following formula so it returns the value Wood:

=VLOOKUP(C6,C2:**G6**,5,0)

3. If the Height column contains our lookup value and Length is the column we plan to use for a return value, what should be our table array?

D2:F6 at a minimum. D2:G6 is also acceptable.

4. If cell I6 contained the value C2:G6 and we wanted to use I6 as a reference, what will our VLOOKUP statement look like if the lookup value is Rustic Root and the column index is 5?

=VLOOKUP("Rustic Root",INDIRECT(I6),5,0)

5. How many columns are in the table array F4:Q34? **12**

6. Why would this formula return an error?

=VLOOKUP(C2,D1:M6,20,0)

The column index, 20 falls outside the table array D through M (10 columns).

7. When and why should we use single quotation marks in a VLOOKUP formula?

When referencing a different worksheet with a name that contains spaces.

8. Based on the table array syntax, is the following a valid VLOOKUP statement? Why or why not?

=VLOOKUP(2,D:Q,3,0)

Yes. The table array references entire columns D through Q.

COLUMN INDEX

The column index is the third argument of the VLOOKUP function. It tells Excel that once my lookup value is found in the leftmost column, move that many cells to the right – on that specific row – to find the answer. The metaphor used earlier illustrates the use of column index best:

If the lookup value describes which floor to press on an elevator, and the table array describes which building we need to be in, the column index tells us what number is on the door.

Column index is the number of columns to count from the left side of the table.

For example, the number 1 as a column index tells Excel to return the value in the first column, meaning the equivalent of the lookup value. When we type this formula into a cell:

=VLOOKUP("OMG",A1:Q17,1,0)

If Excel finds a match in the table array, the cell will populate with OMG.

If we enter the number 2 as a column index, Excel will look one cell to the right of the lookup value.

If I enter the number 7 as a column index, Excel will look six cells to the right of the lookup value.

To state it succinctly: The column index represents x -1 columns from the first column of the table array.

Outlaw Calculations Report

For the next section, use the worksheet named Outlaws.

If we have a table that represents the windows and the floors from which outlaws are shooting, and we want to return the window for a specific outlaw – which is marked by an X – we would need to use this formula:

=VLOOKUP("Doc Holliday",E1:L8,3,0)

This will return an X because Doc is at Window2, which is three columns away from the beginning of the table array. See how this works? It requires counting from the first column to the column with the X.

Outlaw	Window1	Window2	Window3	Window4	Window5	Window6	Window7
Doc Holliday		X					
Jesse James					X		
Billy the Kid							X
Bonnie and Clyde	X						
John Wesley Hardin						X	
Butch Cassidy				X			
Sundance Kid			X				

Figure 21: The Outlaws worksheet

For each of these outlaws, try typing a formula to see if you can return their X.

How did you do? Did you notice that the first column of this table was not column A? That was intentional.

Remember Your ABCs

When determining the column index, especially when the column you are looking to return is far from your lookup value, it is imperative that you know your ABCs. I say this only half-jokingly. There are some concepts that are important in relation to ABCs and Excel:

- **M is the Thirteenth Letter**
  Knowing the number for any letter of the alphabet can be helpful, but knowing that M is the middle letter of the alphabet means we can start at thirteen and work our way backward or forward from there.

- **There are Twenty-Six Letters in the Alphabet**
  While this is a given, knowing how far column AD is from BF, for example, requires thinking about this fact.

- **AA Follows Z**
  The sequence of double lettered columns can make a brain cloudy, so carefully think it through when moving across columns like that.

In addition to those points to consider when counting columns, remember that the lookup value may not be the first column of the worksheet.

If you don't keep these things in mind when formulating a VLOOKUP, you might get confused when entering the column index.

Tricks for Counting Columns

While the earlier information is helpful, there are additional tricks we can use to get the correct column index:

If we use the mouse to select the table array while entering the formula – rather than type it in – a tooltip appears in the bottom right corner of our selection (in the following illustration, it's near cell M9). This table array is eight cells high (R = Rows) and eight cells wide (C = Columns).

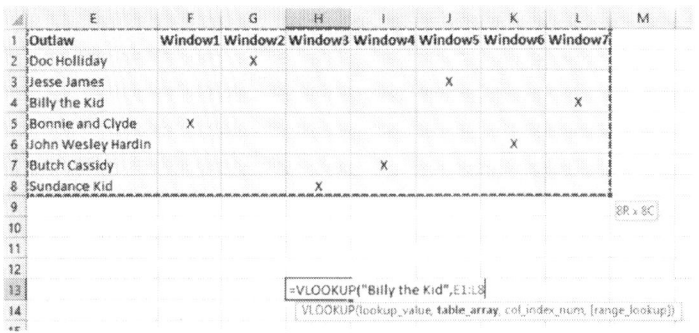

Figure 22: A demonstration of the table array dimensions tooltip

We can select the column headings and see their Count displayed in Excel's status bar, as in the following illustration. This tells us how many cells with data are selected, and therefore, a count of the columns.

Important Note Excel does not include empty cells in this count. Also, if the headings are numeric values, Excel will display their sum, as well. Do not confuse the Count with the Sum. These asides may sound silly, but I have seen them happen.

E	F	G	H	I	J	K	L
Outlaw	Window1	Window2	Window3	Window4	Window5	Window6	Window7
Doc Holliday		X					
Jesse James					X		
Billy the Kid							X
Bonnie and Clyde	X						
John Wesley Hardin						X	
Butch Cassidy				X			
Sundance Kid			X				

Figure 23: A demonstration of selecting column headings to get a column count

We can also use a formula to tell us what our column number is. The COLUMN function accomplishes this. In the following illustration, you see column BI is the sixty-first column on a worksheet.

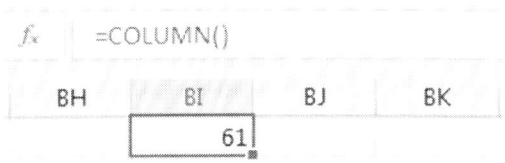

f_x =COLUMN()

BH	BI	BJ	BK
	61		

Figure 24: Using the COLUMN function to display the column's position.

We can create a new Excel file and quickly enter data into the columns we'll need (D through AH, for example), select the cells, and then check their count.

We may even decide to "wing it" and write the formula with the incorrect column index intentionally. Once we review the value displayed, we can compare it to the table array and recalibrate the column index accordingly.

These are all effective strategies for obtaining the correct column index. Soon we will also discuss additional methods for making a column index easier and less about counting.

Using a Header Value

A critical way to use reference values in a column index is a header row or footer row. If we have a row that contains the column index, then we can simply reference it without any need to calculate or count.

For this section, use the worksheet named Jam Sales.

If we wanted to retrieve July's sales for blackberry jam, we could enter the following formula to return the number 8:

=VLOOKUP("Blackberry",A2:M6,H1,0)

Using the reference H1, we can be confident that it will point to the correct column index. Using this type of reference field makes for significantly less work.

	A	B	C	D	E	F	G	H	I	J	K	L	M
1		2	3	4	5	6	7	8	9	10	11	12	13
2	Jam	Jan_Sales	Feb_Sales	Mar_Sales	Apr_Sales	May_Sales	Jun_Sales	Jul_Sales	Aug_Sales	Sep_Sales	Oct_Sales	Nov_Sales	Dec_Sales
3	Strawberry	150	200	204	216	229	243	258	273	224	184	151	174
4	Grape	175	195	235	240	245	250	255	260	213	175	144	173
5	Blackberry	104	137	170	173	175	163	225	245	159	146	109	96
6	Marmalade	136	157	210	177	201	202	228	192	136	108	111	98

Figure 25: The Jam Sales worksheet

Summary

This completes our section on the column index. We covered:

- The column index is equal to x - 1 columns from the lookup column
- The importance of the alphabet in the context of the column index
- Other methods for calculating the column index
- Using a header as a reference value

The next chapter will cover Range, the fourth and final argument in the VLOOKUP function.

Quick Quiz

1. What is the column index when you want the return value to equal the lookup value?

2. The function used to determine the column number of the current cell is _____?

For questions 3 and 4, refer to this mood table:

	C	D	E	F	G	H	I	J	K	L	M	N
1		1	2	3	4	5	6	7	8	9	10	11
2			Jubilant	Stoked	Happy	Content	Ok	Indifferent	Apathetic	Meh	Blue	Depressed
3		Gina							X			
4		Oliver			X							
5		Jerome									X	
6		Oula		X								

3. Using a header value as the column index reference, write the formula that will return X when Gina is the lookup value.

4. What cell would you reference to return the X marking Oula's mood?

Quick Quiz Answers: Column Index

1. What is the column index when you want the return value to equal the lookup value? **1**
2. The function used to determine the column number of the current cell is **COLUMN()**.

For questions 3 and 4, refer to this mood table:

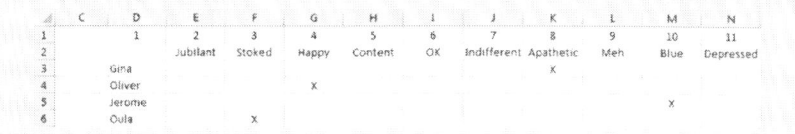

	C	D	E	F	G	H	I	J	K	L	M	N
1		1	2	3	4	5	6	7	8	9	10	11
2			Jubilant	Stoked	Happy	Content	OK	Indifferent	Apathetic	Meh	Blue	Depressed
3		Gina							X			
4		Oliver			X							
5		Jerome									X	
6		Oula			X							

3. Using a header value as the column index reference, write the formula that will return X when Gina is the lookup value.

    =VLOOKUP("Gina",D1:N6,K1,0)

4. What cell would you reference to return the X marking Oula's mood? **F1. The complete formula would read:**

    =VLOOKUP("Oula",D1:N6,F1,0)

RANGE

The fourth argument in the VLOOKUP function is the range. As noted earlier, the range is shown in the formula between brackets ([ ]), suggesting that the argument is optional. What happens if you leave it out? It defaults to 1 or TRUE.

If you have been paying attention up until now, which I hope you have, every VLOOKUP example provided in the book up to this point contains a 0 (zero) or FALSE for the range argument.

```
=VLOOKUP(A2,E1:G9,2,0)
```
VLOOKUP(lookup_value, table_array, col_index_num, [range_lookup])

Figure 26: The range argument is the last piece of the VLOOKUP function

So, then, what is the scenario for using 1 or TRUE, and why would Excel default to that value? While I cannot answer the second question, we will address the first question for most of this section.

For the next section, use the Animal List worksheet.

Microsoft uses the term approximate match when describing the use of range. I find this somewhat misleading because it is not the intuitive wildcard match, where we look for a string with a specific beginning or ending, and the other characters could be anything. For more on wildcard searches, see "Searching with Wildcards" in the Appendix. So what does an approximate match do if we treat it like a wildcard match?

	A	B
1	Animal	Amount
2	Aardvark	27,124
3	Afghan Hound	19,763
4	Albatross	22,691
5	Alligator	56,118
6	Angelfish	30,201
7	Anteater	50,808
8	Antelope	52,849
9	Armadillo	56,111
10	Baboon	41,930
11	Badger	10,000

Figure 27: The Animal List worksheet

When we use the following formula on the preceding table with the assumption that Microsoft's approximate match will return Baboon, we will unexpectedly retrieve Armadillo.

$$=VLOOKUP("Ba",A1:A10,1,1)$$

One may find the range baffling when used this way. Using a 1 or TRUE value for the range will not provide answers typically sought when performing a VLOOKUP.

So what is the correct use for this argument in the VLOOKUP function?

The name of the argument itself – range – gives a more complete understanding of its purpose. Range is used when we need to segment our information. Other common terms for this are histogram, stratify, bucketize, and categorize. Bucketize is not a real word, but you will find it in the jargon of consultants and buzzword propagandists.

With a range argument of 1 or TRUE, we can look at our data and, using VLOOKUP, determine into which "bucket" they fall. We can categorize based on either the numeric or alphabetic value of a lookup value.

Continuing with the Animal List example, if we enter a VLOOKUP with Baboon as the lookup value (by referencing its cell A10), cells E2 through E27 as the table array, and 1 as the column index, the full VLOOKUP formula looks like this:

$$=VLOOKUP(A10,E2:E27,1,1)$$

And the returned value will be B.

Important note E2:E27 references the table array containing the 26 letters of the alphabet, not the list of animals or amounts, as shown in the following illustration.

	A	B	C	D	E
1	Animal	Amount			Alphabet
2	Aardvark	27,124			A
3	Afghan Hound	19,763			B
4	Albatross	22,091			C
5	Alligator	56,118			D
6	Angelfish	30,201			E
7	Anteater	50,808			F
8	Antelope	52,849			G
9	Armadillo	56,111			H
10	Baboon	41,930			I
11	Badger	10,000			J
12	Basset Hound	22,807			K
13	Bat	26,078			L
14	Beagle	33,398			M
15	Beaver	25,016			N

Figure 28: Animal List worksheet with Alphabet column

Unlike our other VLOOKUP uses, a range uses a range table for the table array. There are three rules for setting up the range table:

Rules for Ranges #1: No Gaps

The alphabet from A to Z is the range provided in this example. Note that there are not any gaps in the series. This is important for both alphabetic and numeric ranges.

This is also why our result was Armadillo when we entered the formula:

=VLOOKUP("Ba",A1:A10,1,1)

The animal names are arranged alphabetically, therefore Armadillo is the closest match to Ba, because Ba comes before Baboon. Remember the laziness of VLOOKUP in choosing the first match. That is the driving reason why Armadillo is the result here. That brings us to the second rule...

Rules for Ranges #2: Ascending Order

All values in the segment table must be arranged from smallest to largest, whether alphabetic or numeric.

Rules for Ranges #3: Descriptive Values to the Right

As with all lookup tables, our values must be the first column on the left with the segment names to the right. The VLOOKUP will be used on the range table and the returned value will be the segment name. We will refer to the segment names in the column index. While this did not matter for our Baboon example, it will matter when using descriptive names for segments.

Numeric Ranges

Let's examine segmenting using numeric ranges:

	J	K	L
2	Min >=	Max <	Description
3	0	5000	0 - 5k
4	5000	10000	5 - 10k
5	10000	25000	10k - 25k
6	25000	50000	25k - 50k
7	50000	75000	50k - 75k

Figure 29: A range table example with segment names in the Description column

If we check this table against our three rules for ranges, we'll recognize that this range:
- Has no gaps in the number series (assuming all the values are integers)
- Is arranged in ascending order, smallest to largest
- Has the lookup values to the left of the descriptive column

In addition, our table has a maximum value for each row in column K, but this is optional. We are keeping it there for our reference, but the formula would not be impacted if we deleted that column.

So what does the formula look like?

For Aardvark, where the value for Amount shows 27,124, we type the following formula:

=VLOOKUP(B2,J3:L7,3,1)

The value returned is 25k - 50k.

This makes sense because the contents of cell B2 is 27,124, which falls between the Min >= of 25,000 and the Max< of 50,000. Note that we used a column index of 3 to return the Description column.

Try removing the maximum values in column K to see if the formula still works. Can you see why this is so?

What happens if we break the range rules listed earlier? What impact would it have on the Amount? Experiment with creating gaps, overlapping amounts, and reordering to understand the importance of each of these rules.

Summary

This completes our section on range. We covered:

- When to use a range of 1 or TRUE
- The three range rules – No gaps, Ascending order, and Descriptive values to the right
- Examples of alphabetic and numeric range usage

Now that you have a better understanding of how range works, we have completed the basic coverage of how to use the VLOOKUP arguments. Soon we will move on to more advanced topics – but first, we will look at making mistakes!

Quick Quiz

1. When left blank, the default value for a VLOOKUP range argument is ____.
2. Which of the following is not one of the three rules that apply to range tables?

    A. No gaps between values
    B. Range values must be in ascending order
    C. Each range value must contain a minimum and maximum
    D. Descriptive values for ranges are located at the right

3. True or False: Ranges can be numeric or alphabetical.

Quick Quiz Answers: Range

1. When left blank, the default value for a VLOOKUP range argument is **1**.

2. Which of the following is not one of the three rules that apply to range tables?

    E. No gaps between values
    F. Range values must be in ascending order
    G. Each range value must contain a minimum and maximum
    H. Descriptive values for ranges are located at the right

This is not a rule. The maximum value is not mandatory.

3. True or **False**: Ranges can be numeric or alphabetical

False: Ranges can be numeric or alphabetical.

MAKING MISTAKES – ERROR MESSAGES

Prior to leading one of the largest regional accounting firms in Atlanta, Georgia, one of the senior partners moonlighted as a college professor. His students once asked him how he learned so much. He replied, "I learned a lot of what I know from making mistakes."

Part of learning is taking risks to understand things we do not, and sometimes the result is a mistake. This is failure, and this is good! We need to embrace this kind of failure as a learning experience. Our brains learn critical information and internalize it when we recognize why something went wrong.

While your goal for reading this book may be knowing how to write the 48 (or more) different formats of VLOOKUP functions provided here, I would recommend pushing the limits on the examples provided to see how the formula can break. That experimentation will save you hours of time when you are in the middle of a report that gives an unexpected result.

When pushing limits, it will be helpful to know why something did not work as you expected.

In this chapter, we will look at – and troubleshoot – various error messages VLOOKUP produces when something fails.

#N/A Error

For the next section, use the worksheet named Tallest Buildings, which contains the 10 tallest buildings in the world (as of the printing of this book).

The first error message we will examine is #N/A, a result of the VLOOKUP function when no result is available – this is what N/A stands for: No value is Available.

For example, in our table of the ten tallest buildings in the world, if we typed:

=VLOOKUP("Sears Tower",B1:G11,4,0)

We might expect to find the height of the Sears Tower in Chicago. We will not find it, however, for two reasons:

As of the time of this printing, it is the sixteenth tallest building in the world, and thus outside the top ten.

It has been renamed the Willis Tower, and would not be listed with the Sears name.

We will also get a #N/A error if we typed the following:

=VLOOKUP("Seoul ",C1:G11,3,0)

Because we added a space after the city name Seoul in our formula. Excel was not expecting the extra space, so we still receive #N/A.

	A	B	C	D	E	F	G
1	Rank	Building	City	Country	Height (ft)	Floors	Built
2	1	Burj Khalifa	Dubai	United Arab Emirates	2,717 ft	163	2010
3	2	Shanghai Tower	Shanghai	China	2,073 ft	128	2015
4	3	Abraj Al-Bait Clock Tower	Mecca	Saudi Arabia	1,971 ft	120	2012
5	4	Ping An Finance Centre	Shenzhen	China	1,965 ft	115	2017
6	5	Lotte World Tower	Seoul	South Korea	1,819 ft	123	2016
7	6	One World Trade Center	New York City	United States	1,776 ft	104	2014
8	7	Guangzhou CTF Finance Centre	Guangzhou	China	1,739 ft	111	2016
9	8	Taipei 101	Taipei	Taiwan	1,667 ft	101	2004
10	9	Shanghai World Financial Center	Shanghai	China	1,614 ft	101	2008
11	10	International Commerce Centre	Hong Kong	China	1,588 ft	118	2010

Figure 30: The Tallest Building worksheet

The #N/A result is an ugly reminder that the data we're looking for is simply not available. Whenever this happens, it means either what we are looking for is not there or we are looking in the wrong place.

To troubleshoot this problem, start by checking the lookup value (the first argument) to confirm it is spelled correctly. When inspecting the cell that contains the lookup value, make sure it does not have any stray spaces or other unexpected characters. If you are comparing two numbers, those can prove to be a problem. See the "Cleaning Data" discussion in the Appendix.

One quick way to confirm the lookup value is not the problem is to copy and paste the referenced value into the table array. For example, copy the value Sears Tower from the formula and paste it into cell B2. If #N/A is still the VLOOKUP result, then the problem is not with the first argument.

In a case where the error did not appear to come from the lookup value, check the table array (the second argument). Confirm that the lookup value is the first column of the table array. Also, examine the last row of the table array – is the lookup value located outside of the table array? These are possible reasons the table array is incorrect that will result in a #N/A error.

If you select the cell with the #N/A, you will see colors bordering the cells included in the formula. If the first column of the table array is not the one containing the lookup value, the formula is structured incorrectly. Change the table array to begin on that column and the #N/A error should go away.

Rank	Building	City	Country	Height (ft)	Floors	Built
1	Burj Khalifa	Dubai	United Arab Emirates	2,717 ft	163	2010
2	Shanghai Tower	Shanghai	China	2,073 ft	128	2015
3	Abraj Al-Bait Clock Tower	Mecca	Saudi Arabia	1,971 ft	120	2012
4	Ping An Finance Centre	Shenzhen	China	1,965 ft	115	2017
5	Lotte World Tower	Seoul	South Korea	1,819 ft	123	2016
6	One World Trade Center	New York City	United States	1,776 ft	104	2014
7	Guangzhou CTF Finance Centre	Guangzhou	China	1,739 ft	111	2016
8	Taipei 101	Taipei	Taiwan	1,667 ft	101	2004
9	Shanghai World Financial Center	Shanghai	China	1,614 ft	101	2008
10	International Commerce Centre	Hong Kong	China	1,588 ft	118	2010

Figure 31: An example of #N/A where the lookup value is outside of table array

For example, if we type:

=VLOOKUP("Taipei 101",C3:F10,4,0)

As shown in the preceding illustration, we get a #N/A error because the value Taipei 101 is in column B, however, our table array begins in column C. If we change the table array to B3:F10, we will have corrected the problem.

How would you need to adjust the formula if you were looking for the height of the International Commerce Centre?

#REF! Error

In basketball, football, or soccer, when a ball goes out of bounds, the referee will call it. The same goes for this error. The #REF! error means the reference you are making in your column index argument is outside the bounds of the table array. With the Tallest Buildings table from the earlier, if we entered the formula:

=VLOOKUP(6,A1:C7,4,0)

It will return a #REF! error. How do we know that without looking at it in Excel?

If we recall our ABCs, then we know that counting columns A, B and C arrives at three, but the column index in our formula is 4. We get the #REF! error because we are referencing the fourth column from the lookup value when the table array only contains three columns. To fix this, change the second argument to A1:D7. The result will remove the #REF! error and populate with the contents of cell D7. We could also change the column index to 3 or less.

#VALUE! Error

While a #N/A is the result of an error in the first or second argument, and #REF! signifies a problem in the second or third argument, #VALUE! is sending the message that our formula is syntactically incorrect. This is Excel acting like an English teacher who corrects a student when they ask "Can I go to the bathroom?" instead of "May I go to the bathroom?"

We may understand what we intended with our formula, but Excel is confused (or is pretending to be). If the formula has curly quotation marks (" "), and not straight quotation marks (" "), we will get a #VALUE! error. If our column index is less than one or contains both an integer and a letter, those would also generate this error.

When conducting a troubleshooting exercise on this or any of the other errors, it is best to break down the problem by confirming each part of the formula works in another, simpler formula.

Other Common Pitfalls

Multiple Values
If the same value appears more than once in the column you are looking up, Excel will only return the first occurrence of the value.

#NAME?
Similar to the #VALUE! error – although Excel recognizes the formula, it cannot resolve it using the given argument.

Stray Characters
Data often contains leading spaces or other unwanted, non-printable characters. Several ways to clean your data set prior to performing a VLOOKUP are covered in the "Cleaning Data" section of the Appendix.

Numbers as Text
When the lookup value and the referenced columns don't contain the same type of numbers – one contains numerical values while the other contains numbers used as text. Use Text to Columns to change the format of the value in the column to text. Step-by-step details on how to change numbers to text are available in the "Copying and Pasting Quickly" section of the Appendix.

Date Formats
I strongly recommend against using a VLOOKUP with dates as a lookup value. The frustration, anguish, confusion, and chaos are not worth the effort.

When we type a date or month name into a cell, Excel automatically applies the Date format. If the column containing our lookup value contains a date, it will be difficult to use VLOOKUP because the value within the cell may not be what we think it is.

One possibility is it may be a timestamp, which includes both a date and a time, such as 4/12/2017 15:23:08. If we searched with the string "April 12", no match would be found.

If you must search for a month, a workaround is to add an apostrophe before the value so Excel will interpret it as text, for example: '4 or '04 or 'April.

There are other tricks to formatting dates as non-dates, and I would recommend any strategy that accomplishes this. See Dave Bruns' article

"Convert date to text" for additional help with dates in Excel.

Summary

This completes our section on making mistakes. We covered:
- The importance of making mistakes and what we can learn from them
- #N/A errors and the underlying causes
- #REF! errors and common troubleshooting approaches
- #VALUE! errors and a common syntax mistake
- Other common errors that occur with certain data types in VLOOKUP functions

Making mistakes and learning from them is important. Sometimes, though, we need to remove the noise and keep any errors quiet on a completed report. The next chapter covers that.

Quick Quiz

1. Which error indicates a value cannot be found?

2. How can you confirm an error is not due to an incorrectly-spelled lookup value?

3. Which error indicates a column index greater than the bounds of the table array?

4. Which error indicates a column index less than the bounds of the table array?

Quick Quiz Answers: Making Mistakes – Error Messages

1. Which error indicates a value cannot be found? **#N/A**

2. How can you confirm an error is not due to an incorrectly-spelled lookup value?
   Copy and paste the lookup value into the first column of the table.

3. Which error indicates a column index greater than the bounds of the table array? **#REF!**

4. Which error indicates a column index less than the bounds of the table array? **#VALUE!.**

HANDLING ERRORS GRACEFULLY

When Excel cannot find the value we are seeking, it informs us with an unpleasant-looking message: #N/A. This means the value we seek is not available. It is equivalent to Return to sender in postal speak, mailer-daemon undeliverable in email speak, or 404 file not found in HTTP speak.
I remember playing Concentration as a kid, the card-matching game where you flip over two cards. If the flipped cards match, you get to keep the pair of cards and play another turn. If the cards do not match, then you give up your turn. I also remember the feeling of despair after incorrectly picking and losing my turn. I get a similar feeling when Excel gives me a #N/A.

Sometimes it is unavoidable because not all #N/As are syntax errors. All #N/A's are displayed the same way by Excel, but there are times when the formula is correct and the data we are seeking is simply unavailable.

What if we pulled sales data for our account managers for the first three months of the year, and one of them (Janine) joined in February, so she had no sales recorded in January? This proves problematic when we display the sales information and #N/A is the result for Janine's sales in January – and even for the first quarter – while the sales for February and March display as expected.

Account Manager	Jan	Feb	Mar	Q1
Alfred	$140,824	$292,247	$107,605	$540,676
George	$650,144	$279,831	$258,343	$1,188,318
Janine	#N/A	$502,608	$418,727	#N/A
Total	#N/A	$1,074,686	$784,675	#N/A

Figure 32: #N/A is displayed whenever data is unavailable, even if the formula is correct

If we were to total the first quarter's sales, we would not get the expected $921,335 as a result due to the loathsome #N/A – #N/A is contagious on a spreadsheet. When a value has it and then calculations are performed on that value, any results will also display the #N/A.

Which is really not loathsome, but more of an alert that something is amiss with your data.

Avoiding the #N/A Result

How do we avoid returning a #N/A?

Finding errors is very important when building a report. They can indicate that a formula was formatted incorrectly or arguments are missing. However, once the report is complete and its formulas are checked, these errors do not provide the same value. To navigate around this issue when using VLOOKUP, we can add an IFERROR function around the VLOOKUP function.

IFERROR contains two arguments: the value and the value to return if the first value results in an error. We can encapsulate a VLOOKUP inside an IFERROR function to prevent errors like #N/A from being returned.

For the next section, use the worksheet named Polygons.

To demonstrate how IFERROR works, we will work with the following table:

	A	B
1	Shape	Sides
2	circle	1
3	triangle	3
4	rectangle	4
5	pentagon	5
6	hexagon	6
7	septagon	7
8	octagon	8
9	nonagon	9

Figure 33: The Polygons table

In cell E2, type the following formula:

=IFERROR(VLOOKUP("rectangle",A1:B9,2,0),0)

Then type this formula into cell F2:

=VLOOKUP("rectangle",A1:B9,2,0)

Both cells should display a result of 4.

Now select cell A4 and replace the word rectangle with the word square.

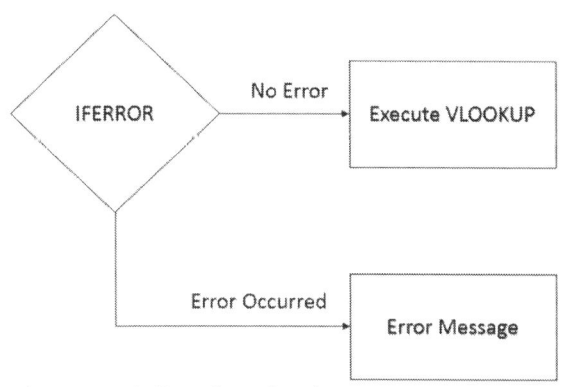

Figure 34: A flowchart for the IFERROR function

We'll find that E2, the cell with the IFERROR formula, responds differently than F2 because IFERROR tells Excel, "If the VLOOKUP function returns something that makes sense, proceed. If not, then make the value 0".

Let's try changing the final 0 in that formula to 42:

=IFERROR(VLOOKUP("rectangle",A1:B9,2,0),42)

Notice how the cell contents change to 42.

Now change the 42 to something else like "THIS CANNOT BE GOOD". Remember, if you use letters instead of numbers, enclose the words within quotations marks. The adjusted formula will look like this:

=IFERROR(VLOOKUP("rectangle",A1:B9,2,0),"THIS CANNOT BE GOOD")

The purpose of the last argument in the IFERROR formula is to instruct Excel what to display if an error occurs. If everything goes according to plan, our VLOOKUP executes. If something goes awry, it returns our error message: THIS CANNOT BE GOOD.

There are also times when numeric values help smooth out the error handling process, as we will see in the next section.

Addition with IFERROR

If we want to pull information from multiple locations and then add them together, we can accomplish this easily using VLOOKUP when the information exists in all locations.

For example, if we have sales for an item in stores and online, each contained in separate places – whether table arrays, worksheets, or files – then we can pull the sales data from both sources and add them together to determine total sales. If only some of the products are available online or not all of the products are sold in stores, then we will have #N/A errors in our VLOOKUP for those items.

For the next section, use the worksheet named Sales Summary.

Figure 35: The Sales Summary worksheet

If we type the following into cell B2:

=VLOOKUP(A2,H1:L8,2,0)+VLOOKUP(A2,H11:L18,2,0)

We will see 900 as the sum of 10 + 890, which is exactly how we want the formula to work. Everything feels like it is coming together, and this report is going to be a breeze – until we reach cell B5 for Item D, where we typed:

=VLOOKUP(A5,H1:L8,2,0)+VLOOKUP(A5,H11:L18,2,0)

The result is a disappointing #N/A because Item D is only sold in stores, not online. Fortunately, we can use IFERROR to successfully add these. When we replace the preceding formula with the following:

=IFERROR(VLOOKUP(A5,H1:L8,2,0),0)+IFERROR(VLOOKUP(A5,H11:L18,2,0),0)

...the result is the equivalent of 0 + 639. Now we can reuse this formula and apply it to all items with satisfying results, including Item W, which has online sales but is not sold in stores.

You can use IFERROR for any mathematical operation you choose to with the same success. Remember that dividing by zero will generate its own error, so keep that in mind for use of division within formulas.

Using IFERROR Rather Than ISNA

Similar to IFERROR is the ISNA function (not available is true) used together with an IF statement. Compare this combination:

=IF(ISNA(VLOOKUP(A4,H11:L18,4,0)),0)

...with the syntax of IFERROR:

=IFERROR(VLOOKUP(A4,H11:L18,4,0),0)

The IFERROR formula contains one fewer set of parentheses. Excessive parentheses, insomnia, fraud, and tax evasion can make life more complicated. I try to keep my life simple, so I prefer IFERROR over IF combined with ISNA. The ISNA formula is apparently a holdover from previous versions of Excel that did not have IFERROR.

Now, if you encounter an IF used with an ISNA formula, you will understand what it accomplishes – the same thing with more parentheses ( ).

A Word of Caution

The IFERROR function is a double-edged sword. While it helps Excel cells play nicely and display cells how we want them to look, it also hides any errors. So, if we expected to see sales numbers for February but we saw a zero, we would have to question that result from a business perspective, but it would not be anything that would raise a flag from an Excel perspective.
I write this because often when you are creating a report, you may want to leave out the IFERRORs until you know the file is working as expected.

Summary

This completes our section on error handling. We covered:
- How to use IFERROR in a VLOOKUP function
- Customizing the error message as numeric or text
- Using IFERROR to perform mathematical operations using VLOOKUPs
- Why IFERROR is better than IF with ISNA
- A word of caution about hiding errors

IFERROR, when used correctly, can replace #N/A with a zero and allow you to add up your report numbers without error. This is a great tool when it comes to VLOOKUP. The next section covers another powerful tool and technique that will save you hours of time.

Quick Quiz

1. What are the arguments of an IFERROR function?

2. Write a formula that returns a total of 2 by adding two IFERROR functions containing VLOOKUP.

3. When is it not a good idea to encapsulate a VLOOKUP inside an IFERROR function?

Quick Quiz Answers: Handling Errors Gracefully

1. What are the arguments of an IFERROR function?
   Value and Value If Error. Value is where the VLOOKUP is embedded, Value If Error is the value returned Excel encounters an error.
2. Write a formula that returns a total of 2 by adding two IFERROR functions containing VLOOKUP

=IFERROR(VLOOKUP("Something",A1:Q232,16,0),1)+IFERROR(VLOOKUP("Something Else",Z1:AF12,14,0),1)

3. When is it not a good idea to encapsulate a VLOOKUP inside an IFERROR function?
   It is best to let error messages present themselves while designing a report, in case the formulas are incorrect.

RELATIVE AND ABSOLUTE REFERENCES

When driving on the highway, when you pass the last rest stop for the next 10 miles, you are progressively moving away from that location. That means no chips, soda, gas, or a bathroom for the next 10 miles.

But if you are driving in a vehicle that has one of the above-listed items in your trunk, then as you drive, these items move with you and their location changes with your relative position – although they are inaccessible unless you stop the car. You could crawl into the trunk through the backseat via the panel behind the armrest of some cars, but I would not recommend this while you are the one driving.

Figure 36: Car moving away from rest area

A referenced value can be relative or absolute. In the case of the snacks, the munchies in the rest area are absolute, while the chips in the trunk are relative to the driver's current position.

Quick sidebar: Most people would prefer shortcuts if they work. One way to accomplish this is through copying and pasting, which saves time.

If we copy and paste a VLOOKUP function from one cell into another cell, and we do not specify that the referenced value is absolute, Excel assumes our reference is relative. It thinks we are in the car together, but, in actuality, we dropped our reference off at the rest area. Essentially, it went to use the bathroom, and I left.

Chicken and Egg

To illustrate this, we will first look at the Chicken Egg worksheet.

The goal here is to copy everything from cells A2 through B4 into cells D2 through E4 while using VLOOKUP.

When we enter the following formula into cell D2, everything matches up the way we expect:

=VLOOKUP(A2,A2:B3,1,0)

	A	B	C	D	E	F
1	Which Came First?	Other				
2	Chicken	Egg		=VLOOKUP(A2,A2:B3,1,0)		
3	Egg	Chicken				

Figure 37: The Chicken Egg worksheet with an effective VLOOKUP formula

If we copy that formula and paste it into cell E2, the formula will read:

=VLOOKUP(B2,B2:C3,1,0)

The result may be what was expected, but look at what VLOOKUP selected for the lookup value and table array:

	A	B	C	D	E	F
1	Which Came First?	Other				
2	Chicken	Egg		Chicken	=VLOOKUP(B2,B2:C3,1,0)	
3	Egg	Chicken				

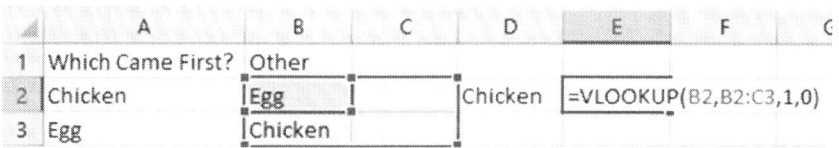

Figure 38: The Chicken Egg table with a VLOOKUP formula that has been mislaid

The lookup value is B2, which shifted one cell to the right from when my

formula was in cell D2. My table array also shifted one cell to the right – from A2:B3 to B2:C3. All of these references are relative.
Let's see what happens when we change one reference to be absolute.
First, delete the contents of cells D2 and E2. Then type the following into D2:

$$=VLOOKUP(\$A2,A2:B3,1,0)$$

Now copy and paste that into cell E2. The result is Chicken, but why? Look at where the lookup value is pointing:

	A	B	C	D	E	F	G
1	Which Came First?	Other					
2	Chicken	Egg		Chicken	=VLOOKUP($A2,B2:C3,1,0)		
3	Egg	Chicken					

Figure 39: With an absolute column reference, the lookup value is now correct

The dollar sign ($) makes the reference to column A absolute, so when we copy and paste the formula into cell E2, the lookup value is still pointing to Chicken in cell A2.

What happens when this spans over several values, and how do we ensure it is set up correctly? We will explore another example to answer those questions.

Rock, Paper, Scissors

To see this happen with more detail, go to the Rock Paper Scissors worksheet.

Once again, we will try to copy the contents of cells A1 through D4 and paste them into cells G2 through I4, using VLOOKUP.

In cell B2, type:

$$=VLOOKUP(A2,F1:I4,2,0)$$

Now select and copy this cell, then paste it into cell C2. Does everything look like it should?

When we select cell B2, we see in the formula that:
- Ref1 is our lookup value

- The table at the right is our table array
- The column index is 2
- The range is 0

	A	B	C	D	E	F	G	H	I
1	Lookup Value	Item 1	Item 2	Item 3		Lookup Value	Item 1	Item 2	Item 3
2	Ref1	=VLOOKUP(A2,F1:I4,2,0)				Ref1	rock	paper	scissors
3	Ref2					Ref2	rock	scissors	chicken nuggets
4	Ref3					Ref3	scissors	rock	candy bar
5		2	3	4					

Figure 40: The Rock Paper Scissors worksheet with an effective VLOOKUP formula in cell B2

Compare that with what happens when we select cell C2. We see:

- Rock is our lookup value
- The table array excludes column F and includes the empty column J
- The column index is still 2, but should it be?
- The range is 0

	A	B	C	D	E	F	G	H	I	J
1	Lookup Value	Item 1	Item 2	Item 3		Lookup Value	Item 1	Item 2	Item 3	
2	Ref1	rock	=VLOOKUP(B2,G1:J4,2,0)			Ref1	rock	paper	scissors	
3	Ref2					Ref2	rock	scissors	chicken nuggets	
4	Ref3					Ref3	scissors	rock	candy bar	
5		2	3	4						

Figure 41: The Rock Paper Scissors worksheet with a misaligned formula in cell C2

So, what went wrong? We told Excel that all the cell references are relative, but some of them need to be absolute.

We will continue to look at how information shifts when using relative references, then we will address how to solve it.

Select and copy cell B2, then select cells B2 through D4 and paste – simultaneously filling all nine cells with the formula. What did you get?

Do cells B2 through D4 match what is in cells G2 through I4? If they do match, then you did not enter the preceding formula precisely. The cell references will shift depending on the cell and, therefore, will result in different values. The following illustrations demonstrate this.

Cell B2 contains our original formula:

Become a VLOOKUP KnowItAll

$$=VLOOKUP(A2,F1:I4,2,0)$$

	A	B	C	D	E	F	G	H	I
1	Lookup Value	Item 1	Item 2	Item 3		Lookup Value	Item 1	Item 2	Item 3
2	Ref1	=VLOOKUP(A2,F1:I4,2,0)				Ref1	rock	paper	scissors
3	Ref2	rock	paper	scissors		Ref2	rock	scissors	chicken nuggets
4	Ref3	scissors	rock	candy bar		Ref3	scissors	rock	candy bar
5		2	3	4					

Figure 42: Our original formula

In cell C2, we see the cells in the formula are shifted one place to the right:

$$=VLOOKUP(B2,G1:J4,2,0)$$

	A	B	C	D	E	F	G	H	I	J
1	Lookup Value	Item 1	Item 2	Item 3		Lookup Value	Item 1	Item 2	Item 3	
2	Ref1	rock	=VLOOKUP(B2,G1:J4,2,0)			Ref1	rock	paper	scissors	
3	Ref2	rock	paper	scissors		Ref2	rock	scissors	chicken nuggets	
4	Ref3	scissors	rock	candy bar		Ref3	scissors	rock	candy bar	
5		2	3	4						

Figure 43: The formula pasted one cell to the right has misplaced arguments

In cell D2, the cells in the formula are shifted one more cell to the right:

$$=VLOOKUP(C2,H1:K4,2,0)$$

	A	B	C	D	E	F	G	H	I	J	K
1	Lookup Value	Item 1	Item 2	Item 3		Lookup Value	Item 1	Item 2	Item 3		
2	Ref1	rock	paper	=VLOOKUP(C2,H1:K4,2,0)		Ref1	rock	paper	scissors		
3	Ref2	rock	paper	scissors		Ref2	rock	scissors	chicken nuggets		
4	Ref3	scissors	rock	candy bar		Ref3	scissors	rock	candy bar		
5		2	3	4							

Figure 44: In the next cell to the right, the arguments have shifted again

If we look at the cells beneath B2, we will see a similar behavior.

Once again, for reference, this is cell B2 with our original formula:

$$=VLOOKUP(A2,F1:I4,2,0)$$

	A	B	C	D	E	F	G	H	I
1	Lookup Value	Item 1	Item 2	Item 3		Lookup Value	Item 1	Item 2	Item 3
2	Ref1	=VLOOKUP(A2,F1:I4,2,0)				Ref1	rock	paper	scissors
3	Ref2	rock	paper	scissors		Ref2	rock	scissors	chicken nuggets
4	Ref3	scissors	rock	candy bar		Ref3	scissors	rock	candy bar
5		2	3	4					

Figure 45: Our original formula

In cell B3, the columns remain constant in the formula, but the row numbers shift:

$$=VLOOKUP(A3,F2:I5,2,0)$$

	A	B	C	D	E	F	G	H	I
1	Lookup Value	Item 1	Item 2	Item 3		Lookup Value	Item 1	Item 2	Item 3
2	Ref1	rock	paper	scissors		Ref1	rock	paper	scissors
3	Ref2	=VLOOKUP(A3,F2:I5,2,0)				Ref2	rock	scissors	chicken nuggets
4	Ref3	scissors	rock	candy bar		Ref3	scissors	rock	candy bar
5			2	3	4				

Figure 46: The formula pasted in the row below has arguments that are also down one row

In cell B4, we see the row numbers have shifted again:

$$=VLOOKUP(A4,F3:I6,2,0)$$

	A	B	C	D	E	F	G	H	I
1	Lookup Value	Item 1	Item 2	Item 3		Lookup Value	Item 1	Item 2	Item 3
2	Ref1	rock	paper	scissors		Ref1	rock	paper	scissors
3	Ref2	rock	paper	scissors		Ref2	rock	scissors	chicken nuggets
4	Ref3	=VLOOKUP(A4,F3:I6,2,0)				Ref3	scissors	rock	candy bar
5			2	3	4				
6									

Figure 47: The formula pasted two rows down has arguments that are also shifted down two rows

One important point evident here is that the inconsistent formula does not affect the value outcome until cell C3! This is critical to understand because, sometimes, if you do not check your formula, you will think you are copying and pasting correctly – you may even spot-check a few cells that look right without even realizing the flaw.

I speak from very personal experience on this. It is unpleasant to work hard on a report that fails to provide the information expected. It is also not good for building credibility and trust with superiors and colleagues on the quality of your work.

So, what can we do differently to keep the references in VLOOKUPs pointing where we want them?

Introducing the Dollar Sign

When designating a value as absolute, a dollar sign ($) is used. When the dollar sign is omitted, the reference will shift as the formula is copied and pasted into other cells. This section will help you understand when and why to use the $, and soon you will understand the flexibility it provides.

As stated earlier, using a dollar sign before referencing a cell's column or row will make that reference absolute (or unchanged). The $ symbol informs Excel that we do not want the reference shifting as we paste the formula into different cells. By adding a $, that reference will not change.

Note that a column, a row, or both column and row can be referenced as either relative or absolute. That means that in one reference, we can keep a row the same (absolute), while the column changes (relative) as we copy and paste from cell to cell.

Now, in cell B2, type the following:

=VLOOKUP($A2,$F$1:$I$4,B$5,0)

Do you see what's happening there?

- In the lookup value argument, A is absolute, while 2 is relative
- In the table array argument, both F and 1, as well as I and 4, are absolute
- In the column index argument, B is relative, while 5 is absolute

When we copy and paste the formula from cell B2 into cells B2 through D4, the values will match G2 through I4. So, how did we do it?

- First, we kept the lookup value's column A absolute so it always refers back to column A on any row or column.

	A	B	C	D	E	F	G	H	I
1	Lookup Value	Item 1	Item 2	Item 3		Lookup Value	Item 1	Item 2	Item 3
2	Ref1	=VLOOKUP($A2,$F$1:$I$4,B$5,0)				Ref1	rock	paper	scissors
3	Ref2	rock	scissors	chicken nuggets		Ref2	rock	scissors	chicken nuggets
4	Ref3	scissors	rock	candy bar		Ref3	scissors	rock	candy bar
5			2	3	4				

Figure 48: An absolute reference to column A

Next, we kept the lookup value's row 2 relative, so it will change as we travel down the table. See cell C3 as a clear demonstration of this.

	A	B	C	D	E	F	G	H	I
1	Lookup Value	Item 1	Item 2	Item 3		Lookup Value	Item 1	Item 2	Item 3
2	Ref1	rock	paper	scissors		Ref1	rock	paper	scissors
3	Ref2	rock	=VLOOKUP($A3,$F$1:$I$4,C$5,0)				rock	scissors	chicken nuggets
4	Ref3	scissors	rock	candy bar		Ref3	scissors	rock	candy bar
5		2	3	4					

Figure 49: An absolute column and relative cell lookup value maintains an effective formula wherever it's placed

- Both the columns and rows of the table array are absolute, so they will remain constant throughout.
- Finally, the column index uses a relative column and an absolute row. Cell B2 has B$5 as the column index. When this is copied, its row will stay the same but the column will shift, as shown in the preceding illustration.

In row 5, cells B through D, we have a footer reference. In a VLOOKUP formula, when we use a literal number as a column index, that value stays the same. But when we use a relative reference, the number will shift as the formula is copied to other columns. By utilizing a footer with a reference as the column index, we won't have to manually adjust this argument in every cell we paste the formula.

Note that while our lookup value has an absolute column reference and a relative row, the column index has the converse – a relative column and an absolute row.

This was a lot to tackle, and we are going to look at a familiar example for our next approach at getting our heads wrapped around absolute and relative references.

Multiplication Table

Consider this old multiplication table from elementary school, available in the worksheet named Multiplication Tables.

Become a VLOOKUP KnowItAll

	A	B	C	D	E	F	G	H	I	J	K	L
1	1	2	3	4	5	6	7	8	9	10	11	12
2	2	4	6	8	10	12	14	16	18	20	22	24
3	3	6	9	12	15	18	21	24	27	30	33	36
4	4	8	12	16	20	24	28	32	36	40	44	48
5	5	10	15	20	25	30	35	40	45	50	55	60
6	6	12	18	24	30	36	42	48	54	60	66	72
7	7	14	21	28	35	42	49	56	63	70	77	84
8	8	16	24	32	40	48	56	64	72	80	88	96
9	9	18	27	36	45	54	63	72	81	90	99	108
10	10	20	30	40	50	60	70	80	90	100	110	120
11	11	22	33	44	55	66	77	88	99	110	121	132
12	12	24	36	48	60	72	84	96	108	120	132	144

Figure 50: The multiplication table with the working area bordered in black

We will attempt to duplicate cells B2 through L12 using VLOOKUP. This will help better explain how the relative and absolute references are interacting as we traverse from cell to cell.

We will use the first column of our multiplication table as the lookup value, the entire table as the table array, and the first row as the column index.

If we enter the following into cell N2, it should display the value 4:

=VLOOKUP(A2,A1:L12,B1,0)

When we copy the formula in N2, select N2 through X12, and then paste, we can see where our formula went wrong. Cell O2 should have a 6, but it shows an 8. This is the result of a relative lookup value that has shifted to cell B2 (with a value of 4).

	N	O	P	Q	R	S	T	U	V	W	X
1											
2	4	8	12	16	20	24	4	12	20	4	20
3	12	21	30	0	30	#REF!	#REF!	#REF!	#REF!	#REF!	#REF!
4	24	40	24	#REF!	#REF!	#REF!	#REF!	#REF!	#REF!	#REF!	#REF!
5	40	0	#REF!	#REF!	#REF!	#REF!	#REF!	#REF!	#REF!	#REF!	#REF!
6	60	#REF!	#REF!	#REF!	#REF!	#REF!	#REF!	#REF!	#REF!	#REF!	#REF!
7	84	#REF!	#REF!	#REF!	#REF!	#REF!	#REF!	#REF!	#REF!	#REF!	#REF!
8	#REF!	#REF!	#REF!	#REF!	#REF!	#REF!	#REF!	#REF!	#REF!	#REF!	#REF!
9	#REF!	#REF!	#REF!	#REF!	#REF!	#REF!	#REF!	#REF!	#REF!	#REF!	#REF!
10	#REF!	#REF!	#REF!	#REF!	#REF!	#REF!	#REF!	#REF!	#REF!	#REF!	#REF!
11	#REF!	#REF!	#REF!	#REF!	#REF!	#REF!	#REF!	#REF!	#REF!	#REF!	#REF!
12	#REF!	#REF!	#REF!	#REF!	#REF!	#REF!	#REF!	#REF!	#REF!	#REF!	#REF!

Figure 51: With a relative lookup value, the formula goes awry in a new location

If we adjust the formula in cell N2 to make the lookup value absolute…

=VLOOKUP($A2,A1:L12,B1,0)

…we can once again copy N2 and paste the formula over cells N2 through X12. And, once again, we see errors in the cells; however, they are different from the errors shown previously.

If we check the formula in cell O2, we now see 4 instead of 6. Now, the table array is still relative, so our lookup value is 2. But the table array has shifted to start in column B, where the number 2 appears in row 1.

Then, based on the column index, Excel moves over three cells to the right and finds the value 4. The logic only gets messier as we look at the formula in other cells.

	N	O	P	Q	R	S	T	U	V	W	X
1											
2	4	4	#N/A	#N/A	#N/A	#N/A	#N/A	#N/A	#N/A	#N/A	#N/A
3	12	#N/A	#N/A	#N/A	#N/A	#N/A	#N/A	#N/A	#N/A	#N/A	#N/A
4	24	#N/A	#N/A	#N/A	#N/A	#N/A	#N/A	#N/A	#N/A	#N/A	#N/A
5	40	#N/A	#N/A	#N/A	#N/A	#N/A	#N/A	#N/A	#N/A	#N/A	#N/A
6	60	#N/A	#N/A	#N/A	#N/A	#N/A	#N/A	#N/A	#N/A	#N/A	#N/A
7	84	#N/A	#N/A	#N/A	#N/A	#N/A	#N/A	#N/A	#N/A	#N/A	#N/A
8	#REF!	#N/A	#N/A	#N/A	#N/A	#N/A	#N/A	#N/A	#N/A	#N/A	#N/A
9	#REF!	#N/A	#N/A	#N/A	#N/A	#N/A	#N/A	#N/A	#N/A	#N/A	#N/A
10	#REF!	#N/A	#N/A	#N/A	#N/A	#N/A	#N/A	#N/A	#N/A	#N/A	#N/A
11	#REF!	#N/A	#N/A	#N/A	#N/A	#N/A	#N/A	#N/A	#N/A	#N/A	#N/A
12	#REF!	#N/A	#N/A	#N/A	#N/A	#N/A	#N/A	#N/A	#N/A	#N/A	#N/A

Figure 52: The problem is not corrected by merely adding an absolute column to the lookup value

So, we will need to rewrite the formula in N2 to make sure both the columns and rows are absolute, to keep the table array constant regardless of where it is referenced:

=VLOOKUP($A2,$A$1:$L$12,B1,0)

Again, copy cell N2 and paste over the previous values in cells N2 through X12.

Become a VLOOKUP KnowItAll

	N	O	P	Q	R	S	T	U	V	W	X
1											
2	4	6	8	10	12	14	16	18	20	22	24
3	12	18	24	30	36	#REF!	#REF!	#REF!	#REF!	#REF!	#REF!
4	24	36	48	#REF!	#REF!	#REF!	#REF!	#REF!	#REF!	#REF!	#REF!
5	40	60	#REF!	#REF!	#REF!	#REF!	#REF!	#REF!	#REF!	#REF!	#REF!
6	60	#REF!	#REF!	#REF!	#REF!	#REF!	#REF!	#REF!	#REF!	#REF!	#REF!
7	84	#REF!	#REF!	#REF!	#REF!	#REF!	#REF!	#REF!	#REF!	#REF!	#REF!
8	#REF!	#REF!	#REF!	#REF!	#REF!	#REF!	#REF!	#REF!	#REF!	#REF!	#REF!
9	#REF!	#REF!	#REF!	#REF!	#REF!	#REF!	#REF!	#REF!	#REF!	#REF!	#REF!
10	#REF!	#REF!	#REF!	#REF!	#REF!	#REF!	#REF!	#REF!	#REF!	#REF!	#REF!
11	#REF!	#REF!	#REF!	#REF!	#REF!	#REF!	#REF!	#REF!	#REF!	#REF!	#REF!
12	#REF!	#REF!	#REF!	#REF!	#REF!	#REF!	#REF!	#REF!	#REF!	#REF!	#REF!

Figure 53: Making the columns and rows of the table array absolute doesn't entirely fix the problem, either

Row 1 of the table looks correct, and if you need to confirm, remember your twos multiplication table.

But row 2 of the table does not make any sense, and based on the reference errors, we can see we need to revise this formula further. Check the formula in cell N3 and you will notice that our column index is not pointing to row 1. We need to adjust the formula to make the row of the column index absolute.

Notice that we do not want to make the column absolute, or we'll see column B repeated eleven times in N2 through X12. The following formula is correct:

=VLOOKUP($A2,$A$1:$L$12,B$1,0)

This formula should replicate the multiplication table from 2 through 12.

I thought this was a great method to demonstrate how the absolute and relative references affect the resulting values. If you need it, I also included a completed version of the multiplication table worksheet as a reference for comparison. Now you may ask, why tell you this here and not earlier? I wanted you to try to figure it out yourself.

Summary

In this chapter, we introduced absolute and relative references. We covered:
- The difference between relative and absolute references
- How their use impacts copying and pasting formulas from one cell to another
- Using the dollar sign ($) to create a reference that will not change

when copied or moved
- How to make an absolute reference for a row, a column, or both

Next, we will cover a powerful function that will help simplify column index usage.

Quick Quiz

In the Column Index chapter, we used the Jam Sales worksheet. Now, using VLOOKUP with relative and absolute references, write a formula for cell B10 that can be copied and pasted into cells B10 through M10 and will contain the full year of marmalade sales.

	A	B	C	D	E	F	G	H	I	J	K	L	M
1		2	3	4	5	6	7	8	9	10	11	12	13
2	Jam	Jan_Sales	Feb_Sales	Mar_Sales	Apr_Sales	May_Sales	Jun_Sales	Jul_Sales	Aug_Sales	Sep_Sales	Oct_Sales	Nov_Sales	Dec_Sales
3	Strawberry	150	200	204	216	229	243	258	273	224	184	151	174
4	Grape	175	195	235	240	245	250	255	260	213	175	144	173
5	Blackberry	104	137	170	173	175	163	225	245	159	146	109	96
6	Marmalade	136	157	210	177	201	202	228	192	136	108	111	98

Quick Quiz Answers: Relative and Absolute References

In the Column Index chapter, we used the Jam Sales worksheet. Now, using VLOOKUP with relative and absolute references, write a formula for cell B10 that can be copied and pasted into cells B10 through M10 and will contain the full year of marmalade sales.

	A	B	C	D	E	F	G	H	I	J	K	L	M
1		2	3	4	5	6	7	8	9	10	11	12	13
2	Jam	Jan_Sales	Feb_Sales	Mar_Sales	Apr_Sales	May_Sales	Jun_Sales	Jul_Sales	Aug_Sales	Sep_Sales	Oct_Sales	Nov_Sales	Dec_Sales
3	Strawberry	150	200	204	216	229	243	258	273	224	184	151	174
4	Grape	175	195	235	240	245	250	255	260	213	175	144	173
5	Blackberry	104	137	170	173	175	163	225	245	159	146	109	96
6	Marmalade	136	157	210	177	201	202	228	192	136	108	111	98

=VLOOKUP($A6,$A$1:$M$6,B$1,0)

THE MATCH FUNCTION

If you have ever ordered your preferred dish from your preferred Chinese takeout restaurant, then you will have no problem understanding the MATCH function.

If I were to order General Tso's Chicken, the person behind the counter would take the menu and circle the number 23 in the column next to my choice. I gave the reference General Tso's, and she identified the number. MATCH works the same way. This function will return an item's position in the given range as a number. Take this grocery list I found in my pocket:

> Thyme
> Hot sauce
> Broccolini
> Wheaties
> Ketchup
> Parsnip
> Quinces

If you are wondering what broccolini is, the MATCH function will not answer that, but I can tell you it is a crossbred vegetable combining broccoli and kai-lan (also known as Chinese broccoli).

What MATCH can tell you is that broccolini is the third item on the list. In Excel, if Thyme was in cell A2 and Quinces was in cell A8, we would represent the function as:

$$=MATCH("Broccolini",A2:A8,0)$$

If we were looking for a needle in a haystack – which I have never done literally, but like to talk about incessantly and figuratively – broccolini is the metaphoric needle, while A2 through A8 is the haystack. The zero in the last argument tells Excel this must be an exact match to broccolini – not asparagus, not broccoli, and certainly not cauliflower.

The preceding formula would return the value 3 because Broccolini is the third item on the list.

MATCH can be done vertically on rows, like we just demonstrated, or horizontally across columns.

If you were a witness to a crime and the police asked you to pick the perpetrator out of a lineup, you might point to the guy with the eye patch, or the guy second from the left, and the police would know you were pointing at number 2. If the lineup were a MATCH function, it would be the following:

=MATCH("Suspect2",H1:L1,0)

	G	H	I	J	K	L
1	Criminal Lineup	Suspect1	Suspect2	Suspect3	Suspect4	Suspect5
2	Name	Lefty Smith	One Eyed Jack	Roy Rotten	Slick Nick	Crooked Charlie

Figure 54: An example of the MATCH function used horizontally

Consider a different example, where we have seven columns with the days of the week, where Sunday is placed in B1, Monday in C1, etc., through Saturday in H1. If we did a MATCH statement like this:

=MATCH("Friday",B1:H1,0)

The result would be 6 – and I would be happy if it was really Friday.

MATCH and VLOOKUP

At this point, you might be asking, "What does this MATCH function have to do with VLOOKUP?"

When the MATCH function is used with VLOOKUP, the combination makes our lookups more powerful. I have seen this referred to as a double lookup or a two-way lookup. So, if anyone asks if you are familiar with those lookup types, your answer is: "Yes, I can write those."
MATCH has a lookup value and a lookup array (a one-line table array). A

MATCH function will return a numeric value indicating the column in the lookup array that contains our lookup value.

We can place the MATCH Function inside VLOOKUP as the column index argument, because that argument expects a number (which MATCH will give us), and we can detect the column we want to use for the column index by feeding MATCH the column header we are seeking.

Runners Club Report

For this section, use the Matching worksheet.

A group of serious, dedicated runners has a planned number of miles to run each week. They track their planned and actual miles using the following chart. Let's say it is now the end of the day on Tuesday, so their actual miles are entered through Tuesday, marked by the dotted line.

	F	G	H	I	J	K	L	M
9		Runners Club						
10	Summary	Sunday	Monday	Tuesday	Wednesday	Thursday	Friday	Saturday
11	John	2.3	3.5	1.5	3	4	0	6
12	April	4	5.2	5.9	4	0	3	7
13	Lucas	2.5	2.5	2	0	2.5	3	3
14	Sam		3.6	4.2	4.5	0	5	6	6

Figure 55: The Runners Club miles tracker

The week-to-date data comes from their actuals table (actual miles run) in cells O17 through V21, while the rest-of-week data will come from their planned table (planned miles to run) in cells O10 through V14. The chart was populated using the MATCH function together with VLOOKUP.

Cell G11 contains the following formula:

=VLOOKUP($F11,$O$17:$V$21,MATCH(G$10,$O$17:$V$17,0),0)

Let's break down that formula...

VLOOKUP function

Lookup value contains an absolute value for column F while the row (11) is relative. This will allow the row to shift as we copy it down to April, Lucas, and Sam while keeping the column constant as we copy across to the columns for Monday and Tuesday.

=VLOOKUP(**$F11**,$O$17:$V$21,MATCH(G$10,$O$17:$V$17,0),0)

Table array contains absolute values for all rows and columns (O17 through V21) to ensure the table array does not shift down or right as we copy and paste cells to other runners and other days.

=VLOOKUP($F11,**$O$17:$V$21**,MATCH(G$10,$O$17:$V$17,0),0)

Column Index contains the MATCH formula that will return the column number.

=VLOOKUP($F11,$O$17:$V$21,**MATCH(G$10,$O$17:$V$17,0)**,0)

MATCH function

Lookup value contains a relative column (G) with an absolute row (10). This will ensure the column always points to the column header.

=VLOOKUP($F11,$O$17:$V$21,MATCH(**G$10**,$O$17:$V$17,0),0)

Lookup array contains an absolute reference to the column headers in the table of actual miles run – O17 through V17.

=VLOOKUP($F11,$O$17:$V$21,MATCH(G$10,**$O$17:$V$17**,0),0)

Match type of zero (0) requires an exact match.

=VLOOKUP($F11,$O$17:$V$21,MATCH(G$10,$O$17:$V$17,**0**),0)

With the MATCH formula complete, here is the VLOOKUP function's final argument:

Range of zero (0) requires an exact match.

=VLOOKUP($F11,$O$17:$V$21,MATCH(G$10,$O$17:$V$17,0),**0**)

Note the absolute and relative references for each of these. The absolute and relative references are structured to make the copying and pasting relatively seamless. Try copying and pasting the formula from G11 through I14.

To enter the formula for the second half of the week – representing the planned miles to run for each participant – use the following formula in cell J11:

=VLOOKUP($F11,$O$10:$V$14,MATCH(G$10,$O$10:$V$10,0),0)

Note the similarities between this formula and the prior one for actual miles run. The only differences are the VLOOKUP table array and the MATCH lookup array arguments.

Now, copy and paste this formula into cells J11 through M14 to complete the table.

Why It Works

Why does this work? We used the MATCH function to tell us what the column index is.

Look at cell G11 for this example:

	F	G	H	I	J	K	L	M
9		Runners Club						
10	Summary	Sunday	Monday	Tuesday	Wednesday	Thursday	Friday	Saturday
11	John	2.3	3.5	1.5	3	4	0	6
12	April	4	5.2	5.9	4	0	3	7
13	Lucas	2.5	2.5	2	0	2.5	3	3
14	Sam	3.6	4.2	4.5	0	5	6	6

Figure 56: The Runners Club miles tracker

=VLOOKUP($F11,$O$17:$V$21,MATCH(G$10,$O$17:$V$17,0),0)

The VLOOKUP function references cell F11 as the lookup value. The table array is the actual miles run in cells O17 through V21. For the column index, instead of providing a value, we use the MATCH function and pass the contents of G10 (Sunday) from the lookup array O17:V17. The MATCH formula counts from cell O17 until it finds the Sunday match in cell P17, and then returns the number 2 for our column index.

Summary

This completes our section on the MATCH function. We covered:
- The definition of MATCH as a function that returns a number providing the position of a specified item in the given range
- Using a MATCH function as the VLOOKUP column index argument to reference table headers and populate the correct data

This was a complex chapter, and it captured various areas from throughout the book. Congratulations on reaching this point!

If you grasp this concept, then you have gained from reading the material in this book. Consider yourself well on your way to becoming a KnowItAll!

The remainder of the material in this book contains other useful VLOOKUP-related information, but the structure of what I set out to convey ends here. I assure you more pieces to this puzzle are provided in later pages. While each chapter up to this point built upon the prior one, the upcoming pages contain more "tips and tricks" type advice.

Quick Quiz

For this question, use the JamVLOOKUP worksheet (not the Jam Sales. The worksheet tab is red to further differentiate):

Using VLOOKUP and MATCH, type a formula in cell B2 for January's Strawberry Jam sales that will match data from the Jam Sales worksheet. Ensure that the formula can be copied and pasted from cells B2 through M5 while maintaining the correct values.

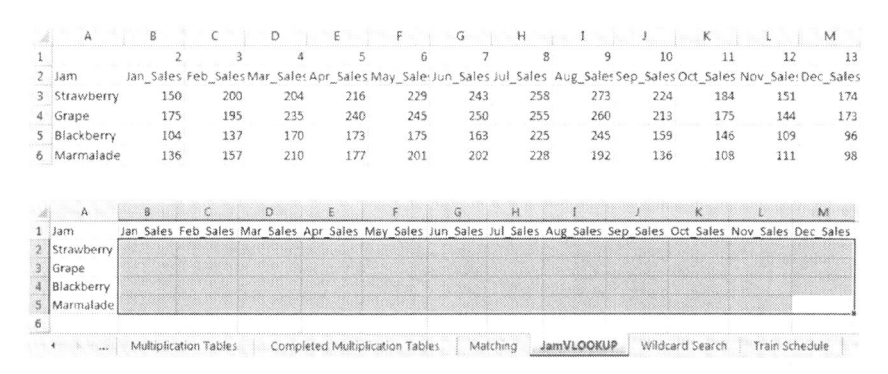

	A	B	C	D	E	F	G	H	I	J	K	L	M
1		2	3	4	5	6	7	8	9	10	11	12	13
2	Jam	Jan_Sales	Feb_Sales	Mar_Sales	Apr_Sales	May_Sales	Jun_Sales	Jul_Sales	Aug_Sales	Sep_Sales	Oct_Sales	Nov_Sales	Dec_Sales
3	Strawberry	150	200	204	216	229	243	258	273	224	184	151	174
4	Grape	175	195	235	240	245	250	255	260	213	175	144	173
5	Blackberry	104	137	170	173	175	163	225	245	159	146	109	96
6	Marmalade	136	157	210	177	201	202	228	192	136	108	111	98

	A	B	C	D	E	F	G	H	I	J	K	L	M
1	Jam	Jan_Sales	Feb_Sales	Mar_Sales	Apr_Sales	May_Sales	Jun_Sales	Jul_Sales	Aug_Sales	Sep_Sales	Oct_Sales	Nov_Sales	Dec_Sales
2	Strawberry												
3	Grape												
4	Blackberry												
5	Marmalade												
6													

Multiplication Tables | Completed Multiplication Tables | Matching | **JamVLOOKUP** | Wildcard Search | Train Schedule

Quick Quiz Answers: The MATCH Function

For this question, use the JamVLOOKUP worksheet (not the Jam Sales worksheet):

Using VLOOKUP and MATCH, type a formula in cell B2 for January's Strawberry Jam sales that will match data from the Jam Sales worksheet. Ensure that the formula can be copied and pasted from cells B2 through M5 while maintaining the correct values.

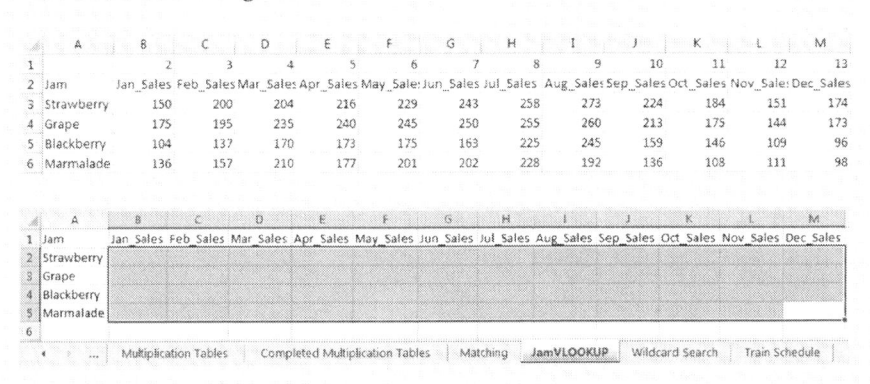

	A	B	C	D	E	F	G	H	I	J	K	L	M
1		2	3	4	5	6	7	8	9	10	11	12	13
2	Jam	Jan_Sales	Feb_Sales	Mar_Sales	Apr_Sales	May_Sales	Jun_Sales	Jul_Sales	Aug_Sales	Sep_Sales	Oct_Sales	Nov_Sales	Dec_Sales
3	Strawberry	150	200	204	216	229	243	258	273	224	184	151	174
4	Grape	175	195	235	240	245	250	255	260	213	175	144	173
5	Blackberry	104	137	170	173	175	163	225	245	159	146	109	96
6	Marmalade	136	157	210	177	201	202	228	192	136	108	111	98

	A	B	C	D	E	F	G	H	I	J	K	L	M
1	Jam	Jan_Sales	Feb_Sales	Mar_Sales	Apr_Sales	May_Sales	Jun_Sales	Jul_Sales	Aug_Sales	Sep_Sales	Oct_Sales	Nov_Sales	Dec_Sales
2	Strawberry												
3	Grape												
4	Blackberry												
5	Marmalade												
6													

=VLOOKUP($A2,'Jam Sales'!$A2:$M6,MATCH(B$1,'Jam Sales'!$A$2:$M$2,0),0)

APPENDIX - OTHER TIPS AND TRICKS

Searching with Wildcards
See the Wildcard Search worksheet for this section.

In card games, we can call a suit or a number wild, like "spades are wild" or "deuces wild". A wildcard search is similar, in that we can look for a match that begins with, or contains part of, what we are seeking without providing the full or exact text.

If we are looking for the word contaminated, and we search conta combined with the wildcard symbol, an asterisk (*) – assembled, it looks like conta* – then we will find contaminated.

In a table where contaminated is in column A...

	A
1	Wildcard Search
2	color
3	clever
4	conserve
5	collate
6	contaminated

Figure 57: The Wildcard Search worksheet

...the complete formula looks like this:

$$=VLOOKUP("conta*",A2:A6,1,0)$$

This works fine unless a word beginning with the same five letters precedes it in the list, such as contain. We know VLOOKUP is lazy. That is one of the basic principles covered at the beginning of the book. VLOOKUP will find the first match and stop. It will not give every match, it will not run a few extra errands, and it will not pick up a latte on the way back. It just finds the first occurrence and nothing else.

If you replaced clever (on line 3) with contain, you would see the formula's result is no longer contaminated.

The wildcard character can be used at the beginning, middle, or end of the string. If we enter the formula:

=VLOOKUP("*c*",A2:A6,1,0)

The result will be color, because the wildcard is seeking a match that begins with, ends with, or contains the letter c.

And if we enter:

=VLOOKUP("*e",A2:A6,1,0)

The result will be conserve. This is because the wildcard says, "Look for any lookup value ending in e."

Another character used for wildcard searches is a question mark (?), which represents any single character. The following formula also returns color, but would never return clever.

=VLOOKUP("c?l?r",A2:A6,1,0)

Cleaning Data

If you are a neat freak, then a speck of dust may drive you insane. I am not obsessive in this manner, although I do get particular about my data – and I have my reasons.

When attempting VLOOKUPs on data containing non-printable characters (or non-blank blanks, as one shop I worked for called them), it can be maddening to be working on a formula, looking for the reason why the cells do not match, only to discover there is a stray space in the value I am looking with. Sometimes this leads to "scrubbing" an entire table.

The best soap I know of consists of this formula. In this example, cell A3 is getting the scrubdown.

=SUBSTITUTE(SUBSTITUTE(CLEAN(TRIM(A3)),CHAR(127),""),CHAR(160),"")

After using the preceding formula, I find my data works well. It removes all the spaces we cannot see with the naked eye. CLEAN and TRIM are basic space-removal formulas. SUBSTITUTE is used here to replace two characters that CLEAN and TRIM do not tackle. CHAR(127) is code for a delete character, while CHAR(160) is a non-breaking space, typically seen in HTML code on web pages.

Using a Column Index Array

There are occasions when we need to obtain multiple cells from VLOOKUP. One method I've found is using an array of column indexes in a VLOOKUP.

We will use the worksheet named Train Schedule for this section.
If we want to add all four values for destination Long Beach into cells H13 through K13, we can do the following:

1. Select cells H13 through K13.
2. Type the following while all four cells are selected:

    =VLOOKUP("Long Beach",A1:D11,{1,2,3,4},0)

3. Now press SHIFT+CTRL+ENTER (a key combination for creating array formulas).

Tip That key combination works for PCs. For the Mac, press SHIFT+⌘+ENTER.

The results populate in the cells selected.

Note the braces { } around the column index argument in the formula, denoting the array members.

Figure 58: Results after adding column index array

Copying and Pasting Quickly

Note Up to this point, most of the book has applied to both Mac and PC versions of Excel. The following keyboard shortcuts have only been confirmed in a Windows setting.

When copying, the easiest keyboard shortcut is to press CTRL+C. When cutting, use CTRL+X. To paste, use CTRL+V.

For additional pasting options, press CTRL+ALT+V to open the Paste Special box.

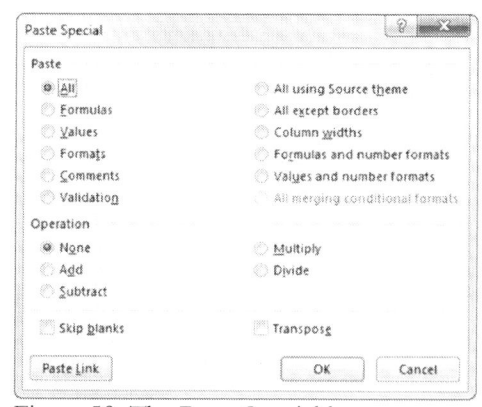

Figure 59: The Paste Special box

Now you can...

- Press F, then ENTER to paste only the formula into a cell and not its results, or

- Press V, then ENTER to paste only values into a cell – the formula's results without the formula, or
- Press T, then and ENTER to paste the formatting of one cell onto another cell without pasting its contents.

These commands will save time when you're trying to paste specific aspects of the copied information.

Converting Numbers to Text

Excel provides several methods to convert a number to text.

One is to click the Home tab on the ribbon, then the arrow at the bottom right of the Number section. The Format Cells box appears and Text is one of the formatting categories available. Once this formatting is applied to a cell, numbers will be treated as text and will display exactly as entered. Also, calculations can no longer be performed on them.

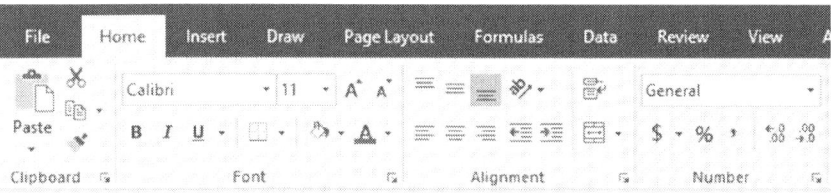

Figure 60: The Number formatting section under the Home tab, at right

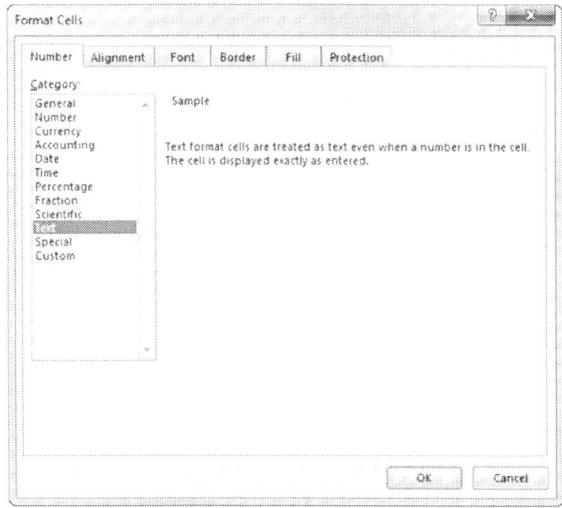

Figure 61: The Format Cells box

This method is not 100% perfect. Altering cell contents can prove more difficult when changing a large set. Additionally, the format can easily change back to Number.

A more reliable method is to place an apostrophe (') before the number in the cell. This method causes the data within the cell to become a text value, not a numeric one.

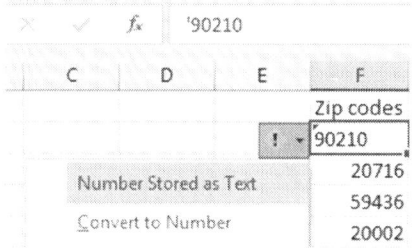

Figure 62: A number preceded by an apostrophe to be stored as text

To accomplish this for multiple rows:
1. Add a column with apostrophes (or single quotation marks), as with Column A in the following illustration.

2. Create a new column (Column B, in this example).

3. Type a concatenation formula that joins the apostrophe column (Column A) with the numeric column (Column C).

4. Copy and paste this formula down the formula column until the last line of data in the numeric column. Here, it would start at cell B2.

5. Finally, select and copy the concatenated results in the formula column, then use paste the values over the numeric column by pressing CTRL+ALT+V to open the Paste Special box, then clicking Values, and OK.

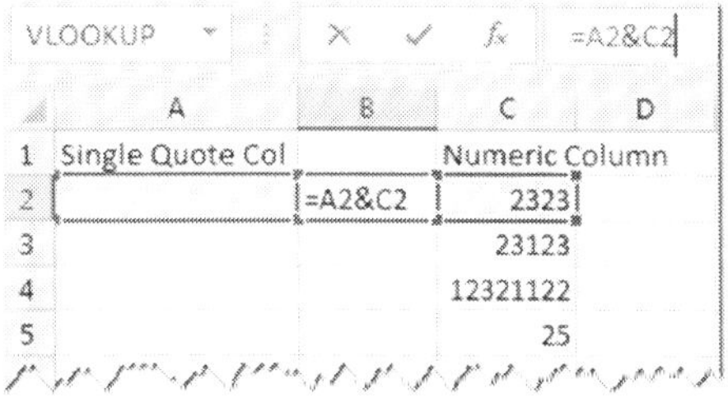

Figure 63: An apostrophe (or single quotation mark) concatenated with numeric values

Is There an HLOOKUP?

This entire book is dedicated to the VLOOKUP function – the vertical lookup. The sister function to VLOOKUP may be HLOOKUP – the horizontal lookup.

The syntax of HLOOKUP is similar to VLOOKUP. It contains similar arguments: the lookup value, table array, row index (instead of a column index), and range. The differences are that the lookup value must be in the first row of the table array, and the column index argument represents the count from the first row.

In my experience, I have used the HLOOKUP function only occasionally. In the business environments I have worked, VLOOKUP has been the standard tool used consistently.

VLOOKUP Usage in VBA

Visual Basic for Applications (VBA) contains a VLOOKUP function. The syntax for using a VLOOKUP function in VBA is unsurprisingly similar to the VLOOKUP function itself:

Application.VLOOKUP(lookup_value, table_array, column_index, range_lookup)

One important drawback when using this function in VBA is the result is not a formula for Excel, only actual values.

I find this to be a drawback because I want to ensure my data is pulling from the location I expect. In this kind of situation, I use a different procedure to populate the cell with a VLOOKUP formula:

myCell.Formula = "=VLOOKUP($H4,$X24:$AC48,3,0)"

This could get more complicated when referencing between worksheets. If I need single quotation marks around worksheet names, I use character code 39 using the syntax: Chr(39).

The full formula would look like this:

myCell.Formula = "=VLOOKUP($H4," & Chr(39) & "Sheet X" & Chr(39) & "!$X24:$AC48,3,0)"

CONCLUSION

This concludes our in-depth review of the VLOOKUP function. We covered the basics and some highly advanced techniques.

If you read this book from cover to cover, understood the material, and worked through the examples presented, you are well on your way to becoming a VLOOKUP KnowItAll. Now, like most skills, it is a matter of practice. The majority of Excel users barely scratch the surface of the VLOOKUP methods described in this book, so congratulate yourself on learning more about this function than the average Excel user.

Do you want to stretch your VLOOKUP even further? Consider learning and incorporating more string manipulation within your data. For starters, master the LEFT, RIGHT, and MID functions. These will help isolate parts of words and numbers.

I hope you enjoyed reading this book. If you would be kind enough to leave a review on Amazon with your feedback, I would be grateful. I also have a blog with additional Excel and analytics-related discussions at

http://notadatascientist.net

Feel free to drop by and browse the material there, as well. I look forward to writing more in-depth reviews and offering material on other Excel-related topics

ABOUT THE AUTHOR

Peter Globus is an MBA graduate and business intelligence professional working with people, business questions, and data. He is passionate about Excel, BI, analytics, and data visualization. His writing explores the depths of analytics topics, the professional use of Microsoft Excel, Power Pivot, Power BI, and analytics software. His first book is on the VLOOKUP function.

Made in the USA
Lexington, KY
21 May 2018